A Home to Cherish

(Create Your Stylish & Healthy Home)

GWENDOLINE ALDERTON

Powerhouse Publications
Suite 124. 94 London Road
Headington, Oxford
OX3 9FN

www.powerhousepublishing.com

In remembrance of my father's love and dedication to his family
W.H. Bibby
(09 Mar 1939 – 15 Feb 2000)

TABLE OF CONTENTS

A NOTE FROM GWENDOLINE

Welcome to a collection of my personal stories: stories to help you understand how to create your stylish and healthy home, stories that showcase the emotional side of interiors and also, why and how I changed career to become an interior designer.

Becoming an interior designer wasn't an obvious choice for me, certainly not something that was planned or my life's ambition. It began with a pivotal moment, when the death of my father collided with the birth of my son, and is what I now refer to as my *Memory to Cherish*. It gave me the impetus to start the journey towards a new career, helping others.

Each story has contributed to my interior design journey. Each one reflects on the emotional side of interior design, connecting interiors with wellness, focusing on major life events. Each one identifies how interior design can create a stylish home, whilst supporting and nurturing a healthier and happier lifestyle.

I also reflect on how dated and disorganised décor can quickly and easily create physical, emotional or mental stress that could lead to lack of sleep, anxiety, poor concentration, sadness, depression, as well as feelings of isolation.

In this book, I'll take you on my journey thorough interiors. With my design expertise and personal experiences, I'll help you understand how to overcome each situation with a stylish and healthy space. If you change your environment, then you have the opportunity to alter how you feel. You can create a happy and healthy space that will enable you to relax and unwind, it can make you feel safe and secure, and it will also energise and invigorate you. It will provide the perfect space to create your own precious memories to cherish. Memories that make you feel loved, uplifted and joyful.

Your life is reflected in your home. If you cherish your home then it will love you back.

Gwendoline x

INTRODUCTION

For the last five years, my resolution was always to write a book. Initially I was writing a 'how to' coffee table book on interior design, full of glossy photos showing amazing rooms. I'd started many editions that lay dormant on my desk. Looking back, I think they were never finished because they didn't contain my heart. I never got further than the first paragraph because I was focused on the theory of interior design, but I was travelling on a journey to connect interiors with emotions, health and happiness.

A Home to Cherish shows the emotional connection with interiors. When emotion is at the heart of your interior, it will help you create a home that focuses on wellness. Connecting interiors with wellness brings a deeper level of personality and individuality to your interior. It creates a space that not only looks good, but also one that feels comfortable and secure, helping you to relax and feel invigorated every day; a space that you want to share with loved ones for a happy and fulfilled life.

Each chapter contains personal interior design stories that are balanced with my professional advice and guidance to support and nurture significant times of life. I share with you how to create a stylish and healthy space with memories to cherish.

Memories to Cherish are positive memories that you can share with others; moments created in the past that can be called upon in the future. Each moment is so very precious because you never know when that memory will be the last and cherished forever. The memories are uplifting and energising when you're feeling weary, comforting and nurturing when you're feeling sad, and a ray of hope when you're feeling lost. They give you the strength to cope when days are challenging, where you might need additional support and encouragement. They help you through the tough times.

You can read the stories in any order but I recommend that you start with *My Story*. It will help you understand why memories to cherish are so very important to me and are at the heart of this book.

All of my stories are based on real situations, with names changed for privacy. There are no pictures in this book because it focuses on stories for the imagination. If, however, you would like a little visual inspiration, then you can link to my website for images of the interiors and my designs: **www.ga-interiors.co.uk/books/hometocherish**

My stories cover a combination of high-end interior design and quick makeover House Doctor projects, so the interiors don't always include luxury, bespoke, rich-looking stuff. They show everyday homes that can be made to look lovely and promote a healthy lifestyle. Once a space is decorated to suit you and your personality, it will reduce stress and save you time because it's organised for your lifestyle. It will make you happy because it feels safe and secure, and it will energise you because it feels comfortable.

The point is to create a home that's individual and unique to you, focused on emotions that elevate your interior from a space that just looks nice, to being a home that looks amazing and, most importantly, feels fantastic.

MY STORY

MEMORIES TO CHERISH

I would like to share with you my 'memory to cherish' that was a defining moment and changed my life forever. It's my story of how the saddest of times created my most treasured memory, and how that gave me the impetus to become an interior designer.

It was the day that my father phoned. That in itself was unusual because it was always my mum that phoned, regular as clockwork every Wednesday evening. I could tell by his shaking voice that what he had to say was major, big stuff. He said, "I've got cancer, it's inoperable and I haven't got long to live."

Shock seems such an understated word for how I was feeling, but I was in absolute shock. My stomach was convulsing, I was finding it difficult to breathe and my heart was about to break.

It was late in the evening: my two-year-old daughter was sleeping soundly and my husband was still at work. I wanted to leave now, to run into the arms of my father, but I knew that we would have to wait until the morning. At three in the morning, my daughter slid into bed next to me for mummy cuddles. As she nestled into my warmth, I felt a gnawing and agonising pain in the pit of my stomach.

When daylight shone through the curtains, clothes started to fly around the bedroom as I packed my suitcase in haste. Even remembering it now, I can see my daughter dancing merrily around the room, excited about going to see Grandad. How was I going to tell her that this was the last time she would see her beloved grandfather?

With the cases packed, hubby and daughter in the car, we were driving along the motorway. But, instead of driving to see my father, we were heading in the opposite direction, straight to hospital.

Aaaargh!!! How could this be happening to me?

I was eight months pregnant and my baby had decided that now would be a great time to make an appearance. I didn't know which was worse, the pain in my belly or the ache in my heart. I remember thinking:

- What if I never see my father alive again?
- What if I never feel his warm embrace?
- What if I never hear him tell me he loves me, just one more time, just one last time?

My thoughts were with my father as every second might be a second too late. I had to get out of the hospital as quickly as possible. I remember thinking, *can't we bung it back in or stitch it up?* Fear and dread kicked in, and I have never pushed so hard in all my life. My baby shot out like a missile on a mission. When the midwife proudly announced, "It's a boy", tears tumbled down my face onto my son's soft wrinkly skin.

Surely we could leave now. No, I was trapped by physical complications. I felt so frustrated and I wanted to weep forever. Would I ever see my father alive again? I just wanted to take my baby and run to my father.

This was the happiest and saddest time of my life with my emotions torn apart. I was supposed to feel overjoyed, having given birth to a beautiful, healthy son but I felt totally crushed. The worry was all-consuming.

I was surrounded by happy people with balloons, flowers and new-born nappy packs. I wanted to scream at them to leave but I suppose it wasn't them that I wanted to leave; it was me who wanted to go.

I had to get out of the hospital. I couldn't wait for my body to get better because I didn't have time on my side. I pleaded with the medical staff to get me discharged. My sister was a nurse and could look after me. She's a children's nurse, not a midwife, but surely that's just details when time is of the essence. My sister, Deborah, was at home nursing my father through his cancer. She was a trooper and I'm grateful she took control of his medical care because I wouldn't have had a clue what to do. I can't even get a plaster to stick on properly.

The car journey was incredibly painful both physically and emotionally. That was all forgotten as soon as I arrived outside the family home. I could finally see my father. As we pulled up outside my parents' home, the car door was thrown open and an arm reached in to grab my baby. Spinning my head around, I saw the back of my sister, Deborah, running up the front steps to the house with my baby nestled in her arms. She was so quick that I hadn't even had time to unbuckle my seat belt.

What did her actions mean? Was it my father's final moment and she wanted him to see his grandson before he took his last breath? These worrying thoughts in my head were quadrupled because I couldn't physically run up the front steps in my condition. Every step ached. What if I didn't make it in time to tell my father that I loved him? What if I'd made it this far only to find that I was too late?

Familiarity comforted me as I passed through the long slender hallway with its swirling patterned carpet. Fond memories occupied my thoughts and I looked to the kitchen door where my mother greeted me with outstretched arms every time I arrived home.

She wasn't there today. I thought, 'Oh no, this is it; she's obviously soothing my father in his final moments.' My heart was beating so rapidly that I could hardly breathe, let alone move. I felt as if I was in slow motion but had to keep moving. Was I too late?

As I stepped into the lounge I saw a picture postcard of my family. My mother knelt on the floor smiling adorably at my son in her lap. It was a moment of comfort for them both. My father was weak but with the little strength he had, he stretched forwards to reach a toy for my daughter to play with. I could see the pain in his face as he reached out with his once powerful and muscular arms. The strength that used to throw us up and catch us so securely had been stripped of all its power. The veins that used to throb with life now dwindled in existence.

I hugged my father so tightly. I'd finally made it in time. My fondest memory of those last few hours was my father holding my son for the first and last time – my father William at the end of his life and my son William at the beginning of his.

It was at that moment that I realised the importance of memories, Memories to Cherish.

As Steve Jobs, co-founder of Apple, who died of cancer aged 56, said, "I reached the pinnacle of success in the business world. In others' eyes my life is an epitome of success... I realize that all the recognition and wealth that I took so much pride in, have paled and become meaningless in the face of impending death. Whichever stage of life we are at right now, with time, we will face the day when the curtain comes down. Treasure love for your family, love for your spouse, love for yourself... Cherish others. When you have mates, buddies and old friends, brothers and sisters, who you chat with, laugh with, have sing songs with... that is true happiness."

When the people you care about are no longer present, you can feel nurtured in their love and affection through the memories you created together. You remember the good times and the happiness shared together. Creating a healthy home promotes happy times and memories to cherish, which in turn helps you get through difficult times.

A CHANGE IN DIRECTION

How would I cope with the grief when I was feeling so deeply wounded? How was I supposed to pick myself up and keep going when the loss was all-consuming? But most importantly, how could I embrace the love for my son when he reminded me of the trauma and the pain of losing my father?

It's now 18 years later and I can remember every moment vividly, from my son's birth until my father's passing, as if it is a film constantly playing in my head.

They say that time heals, but it doesn't. That's just a ruse to try to get you to stop wallowing in the misery, a hope that things will improve and you won't be left feeling so helpless and abandoned. I agree that you have to do something, to learn how to cope with your emotions and move forwards. It doesn't help to put your emotions in a box and try to ignore them. I had to learn how to find the positive because my father wouldn't have wanted me to feel sad. He would want me to live a life full of love and happiness.

Over the years, I've learnt to manage the grief shark by channelling my sadness into creativity. It helps me to relax, clears my thoughts and is a practical way to express my emotions. I've been creative from an early age, but I made things consciously rather than letting my emotions inspire my creativity.

When I was four, before I started school, I spent the summer with my grandma. She was soft and round with a sunshine face that was framed with short, silver-grey, curly hair. Her floral cotton dress had short sleeves, allowing the excess skin on her arms room to wobble as she moved. She was always a practical woman with a frilly apron tied neatly around her waist, with a pocket for a tissue and her tape measure. Every morning she would pop to Mass at the local church and then come home to prepare the dinner for the day, screaming at her kids (my aunts and uncles) to help her sort the house out. She was frequently screaming at them with a furrowed brow, but to me she was soft and gentle with a loving smile.

To me she was the most affectionate and caring person who made me feel secure, who made me laugh constantly and gave me the confidence to be experimental.

I was only supposed to be with her on a two-week family holiday, but I didn't want to go home. I wanted to stay with my grandma in Dublin, and she wanted us to be together. At the end of our holiday, my grandma asked my mother if I could stay a little longer with her. I looked at my mother with hope and she said yes. I burst with joy at the prospect. I felt so very special and overjoyed because I knew it was an adventure waiting to happen.

My grandma lived in a two-bedroom terraced house where she'd raised her six children. She was a single parent after my grandpa died of diabetes when in his prime. Although life was a struggle, my grandma's house was always exciting. The moment you entered the hall there was a door to a private room that we weren't allowed into. It was the parlour for posh people who came to visit. Although no posh people ever came to visit whilst I was there, I imagined they would sit in their colourful finery sipping tea from Grandma's favourite china cups. Grandma would take off her flour-stained apron to reveal her floral silk dress and then walk ceremoniously into the room with her freshly-baked scones.

I suppose she needed a room of calm because as soon as you stepped into the living room you were smacked with real life. It was one large room with a roaring fire and bursting with memories. The sofa was brown, floral and silky, styled with a fur hide over the back. I hated the animal throw because it was hard and scratchy, but it was fashionable and I imagined it was a trophy from an uncle in the country. I preferred to sit on Grandma's chair that was soft and warming. It was a high-backed chair with softly rounded wooden arms, and a collection of padded cushions that kept the mould of her womanly shape whenever she got up.

In a corner of the room was a rainbow of trophies, many of which were taller than me, and topped with motorbike symbols. My uncles were talented at motorbike scrambling, winning plenty of competitions. There were odd bits of bikes and parts in mid-assembly lying around Grandma's house. She always tried to keep the boys in check by hollering at them to clear the table of their dirty oily motorbike parts, so that she could set the table for dinner. It was always fun but chaotic watching the drama of life unfold as the 'workbench' for emergency bike repairs transformed into a nurturing place for the family.

It was at that same table that Grandma taught me to sew, to create and design outfits. It was magical and the most precious time that we shared together, just the two of us. I'd always been used to doing things with my sisters, so it felt very special to have all of her attention to myself. With a whir of the machine and a sparkle in her eyes, we would create the most beautiful dresses.

First thing in the morning, we would pop to the market and hunt out the fabric stall. Her feet would quicken as we got closer and the kaleidoscope of patterns, colours and textures stretched out before us. It was our treasure trove. My grandma explained the different fabrics to me and how they moved – from the gentle flow of luxurious silk to the stiffness of pure cotton and the warmth of woollen tartan. Even today I can't stop myself from touching fabric and feeling its energy because it's such a sweet shop of textures to invigorate the senses.

My mother always fondly recounted stories of my excursions with Grandma, trawling every material shop in the city. On one particular day, after I'd returned to Lancashire, when I got home from shopping at the market with my mother, I collapsed on the sofa in exhaustion and exclaimed, in my new Dublin accent, "Jesus, Mary and Holy Saint Joseph, my feckin' feet are killing me." My mother was shocked and could hear Grandma's voice echo in the room. It makes me smile, thinking of how my mother and Grandma had a chuckle together.

Grandma was the spark for my creativity and when I returned to England there was no stopping me and a pair of scissors. When I heard my mother screaming my name from upstairs, I knew my secret had been discovered. Every step I took up the stairs filled me with dread, but I knew what to expect and I had to tell the truth because there was going to be no way that I could cover this up. How was I going to explain my way out of this?

When I opened the bedroom door my mother was standing in the middle of the room holding a large, white, crisp, cotton sheet. Her furious face was poking through the great big hole that I'd cut in the cloth!

My mother used to recount this story to family and friends for their amusement. Time after time, she would describe her absolute astonishment at finding 'the hole'. Not only was she astonished but also in absolute awe of how precise my cutting was, in a perfect square, so that when the bed was made and the sheet tucked under, you would never have guessed that a whole corner was missing. It was one of my mother's memories to cherish.

As I stood shaking in front of my mother, my only explanation was, "My Barbie doll needed a wedding dress and only the best cotton would be good enough."

Just wait until she checked the rest of her sheets. This was just the tip of the iceberg, and I was soon going to be in serious trouble. You can't make the perfect wedding dress without some experimentation, without a bit of trial and error. Mum always had the finest cotton sheets, but some of the fabric was old and worn so it didn't hang properly. Finding the ultimate cotton sheet was a process of taking a sample from three sheets, cutting off a corner to see how the material flowed. Barbie was marrying Ken and I wanted it to be the most perfect day.

After my mum got over the shock, and my scissors were banned for a month, she asked my father to bring home scraps of material from the textile factory where he worked. 'Great, now I had fabric to make bedding for Barbie's honeymoon suite,' I thought. Working with my hands, being experimental and imaginative with material was always such fun. It was my first flourish into creativity where I consciously began to understand texture, structure and form. I started to appreciate the knowledge and skills that my grandma had nurtured in me.

At the age of sixteen, my grandmother was again my inspiration, but this time it was for a deeper creativity, my inner voice. Something I never knew existed within me.

I don't know how you spent your sixteenth birthday, but I remember being surrounded by my family in a large draughty building with music floating in the background. I was squashed between two aunts, sitting on a cold wooden bench, staring directly at my grandmother's coffin. It was another momentous occasion because my grandmother was my rock, my comfort and my hero. I was absolutely devastated by her death. I always thought that she would live forever. I didn't want to let her go because I loved her so much. I loved all of her cuddles and her soft squidgy bits.

My grandmother was my inspiration, and losing her made this feel like the worst birthday ever. My sweet sixteen! I wondered if my birthday would be totally forgotten, but, of course, a mother never forgets. With all of the distraction and the Irish clan filling the church, my mother quietly hugged me and wished me happy birthday. For her to give me that moment of affection, at a time when she was facing the loss of her own mother, made me feel so very special. It was the best birthday present and a memory I will always cherish.

I was dreading going back to school and facing my friends. How could they understand my grief when their world focused on lip gloss and boy bands? I became quite insular and couldn't talk to my friends because I had nothing happy to say to them. I also didn't know what to say because I didn't know how to express the level of emotion I was feeling. I felt as if I was in my own bubble where life continued and revolved around me even though my heart had been crushed, so I started to write. It felt quite natural and helped me come to terms with my thoughts and emotions, to make sense of a world without my treasured grandmother.

'Little Old Me' was the poem that I wrote as a tribute to my grandmother. With a constant stream of tears, it took me weeks of writing and rewriting. I would write in secret because it was my time to connect with my grief and my feelings, remembering the love of my grandmother. I never intended to write the poem but it just came out as my inner voice, my subconscious thoughts. It helped me explore my emotions and externalise my thoughts. Connecting with my inner creativity helped me produce something personal as a way of dealing with a difficult and deeply sad time.

LITTLE OLD ME
by Gwendoline Alderton (age 16)

The years have gone,
They've passed away,
But here I am the same old way.
My teeth have gone,
My hair is grey,
My children they have moved away.

When I wake up I see the sun;
Another day has just begun.
I look at myself and see the scars
The years have left from the ugly wars.
It's raining now and it's windy too,
The weather can change like me and you.

My husband's gone, he went this year.
When I think of him I shed a tear.
He was kind, gentle, witty and gay.
Why has he gone?
Why couldn't he stay?

There's only me here,
Little old me.
There's only one person to have her tea.
I'll be going soon,
I'll pass away.
I'll visit my husband and there I'll stay.

Years later, when my father died, I needed to find my inner voice again because I felt abandoned. He was my spark and my inspiration. He was the unpredictability in my life that made it exciting and fun. He gave me permission to be me, to be creative and inventive, to be carefree and imaginative. Now that the spark of my father was gone, I needed something that would allow me to express my feelings.

I decided to try and ease my emotions by learning something new, something creative and something that would fit into the only free time I had, whilst breastfeeding my baby. With William nuzzled in my softness, we would both be learning and growing.

An interior design home study course sounded like a good option because it was completely different to my technical career in computing. It sounded colourful, exciting and adventurous – all of the things that I missed about my father. It would allow me to escape into another world, at least for a moment, where I didn't have to remember the loss, experience the pain, or hear the silence now that my father was gone.

Little did I know how that one decision to study interior design would change my life forever; I just thought it would be useful for fluffing cushions. Opportunities aren't always obvious. They don't come with a warning sign saying, "Watch out, this will blow your mind and take you in a new direction." They don't always happen when life is feeling wonderful but they often create a monumental change in direction.

When you take a step forwards, there's no turning back.

STEPPING FORWARDS

Sometimes stepping forwards and taking a risk is the only choice. Staying in the same spot is not an option because you're no longer that person. This was exactly where I was standing, no longer the person I used to be and not knowing the person I was to become. The whole experience of losing my father so abruptly, whilst my son was born so suddenly, had shaken my thoughts, my dreams and my goals.

As I write these feelings, I have goosebumps on my arms because I can hear my father's final words ring clearly in my head; words that would change my perception and refocus my priorities. Words that would fill me with courage to take a step forwards with no turning back.

It was Valentine's Day and my father asked my sister Deborah to buy red roses for my mother, Aedine. My parents brought us up with love and affection, which never waned just because he was riddled with disease.

Lying on the bed, surrounded by close family, my father was asked if he had any regrets. We all waited anxiously because the last thing we wanted to hear was that the person we loved most dearly wished the life he lived was different. There was no time to change things. There was no time to make things better for him. In fact, there was no time left at all.

Why was this question even being asked at a time like this? "Do you have any regrets?" is one of those questions that's only asked when big, important stuff has happened – like when you emigrate to another country, when you finish with a partner or when death is knocking at your door. It was so distressing standing there, thinking that my father might die an unhappy man. I hoped his answer would be blissfully happy, but I felt anxious and totally helpless waiting for his reply.

As we waited for his answer, we were surrounded by the familiarity of the lounge that was oozing family memories. All of our happiness and sadness bottled in one room. I remembered the hours we would sit snuggled together watching old movies, with dad making a brew during the ad breaks. He made a good cup of tea and whenever we were sad, no words were said, he'd just pop the kettle on. It was his way of showing affection.

The one and only time that I saw my father crying was just after his step-father died of cancer. I came down one morning to hear my father sobbing, sitting on the sofa with a brew in hand, nuzzled in my mother's embrace. My mother looked me straight in the eye so that I knew it was a moment of privacy. I went to my bedroom and cried because we'd been waiting for this day.

Having been through cancer with my step-grandfather, we knew the stages and were aware of what was happening, but it was still shocking and unbearable. As we listened to the clock softly ticking away in the background, with nobody wanting to say anything, we waited silently for my father's reply.

My father lay drained and exhausted on the double bed that had replaced the sofa. I didn't know where the sofa had disappeared to. At the time, it was just gone and my mother had dressed the bed simply in her favourite white cotton sheets, (without any holes in them this time). The lounge had become a bedroom where my father could rest, where friends could pay their last respects and where the family felt comfortable.

As my father looked up, I could see his anguished face. He said,

"I've no regrets. I've got Aedine and the girls." To my father, the family unit was paramount. We were his pride and joy. Life was fulfilled as he took his last breath surrounded by the love of his wife and his daughters – his parting memory to cherish.

As I was standing there proudly, feeling loved amongst my family, together in our grief, it reminded me of the saying: love will conquer all. I know that it sounds cheesy but at the end of the day, when there's nothing else to say and do, you want to feel as if you've made a difference by leaving your joy and happiness, your cherished memories, with those you love and care about.

Hearing those words from my father put optimism and hope in my heart. No matter how much sadness, how much pain and how much grief I was feeling, I knew that I had to take his inspiration, his strength and his courage to step forwards. I didn't know what I was going to do or what the steps would be, but I knew my heart was taking me in a new direction.

FINDING THE WAY

Being struck with so many opposing emotions at once was overwhelming, and a thousand questions came to mind. Don't worry, I'm not going to list them all. The important question is always, 'What do I do?'

Now that my father was gone, I was feeling confused and despondent. I was catapulted into self-doubt and uncertainty. I'd never experienced anything like this before. I'd always been the type of person with a clear direction and ambition, but my goals became unclear and I was feeling lost. I was running on autopilot: get up, see to my children, go to work, come home and collapse. I was distracted by everyday living, but it wasn't helping me face my emotions. I needed to take a step off the rollercoaster of life and face the grief shark.

I'd never taken any time to stop. From the very first day my father dropped me off at the school gates, I was always moving forwards, challenging myself and learning new skills. I wasn't stretching myself to be the best, the most famous or the most popular; I just loved to learn. I enjoyed the creativity of learning and the uncertainty of where it might take me. I enjoyed concepts, theories and experimentation. I still do.

Although I'd always found it exciting being challenged and trying something new, maybe now was the time to stop and take some downtime. My father's thoughts of 'family first' had made a significant impression on me; that I shouldn't give all of my energy to my career, but should share time with my family. Maybe now was the opportunity to balance my life instead of working flat out for success. Perhaps success wasn't being a high achiever, and I could try something new, a more even compromise of work and family lifestyle.

Although my career in computing was rewarding, it was also terrible for family life. Working extended hours and evenings, I was then spending my precious weekends catching up and had little quality time with my family. I wanted more time with my children, to share their passions and to stop feeling as if everything I did was compromised. I never felt guilty about putting my children in nursery whilst I worked, although my mother disagreed with my choice of childcare, but I did feel as if I was stretching myself to be constantly 'perfect'. The grief, work commitments and family responsibilities were starting to become overwhelming. I was always running from here to there with a long list of things to do trailing alongside me. Looking back now, maybe it was my way of blocking out the grief; to keep myself busy.

There was one incident in particular that gave me a wake-up call. It was the morning that I walked into the office, blurry-eyed, with my blouse on back to front and inside out. I didn't even notice until my manager mentioned it in the lift on our way to a client meeting. It made me realise that something had to change before I lost all focus and sanity.

I realised that, after 16 years of building up my profession in computing, I now had to let it go and alter my direction, to take a step forwards on a new path. I didn't know what I was going to do, but, writing this now, I realise that I was searching for a journey that would honour my father's memory, something that would take me towards memories to cherish. I was on a journey that would help me through my own grief whilst making a difference to others.

I was fortunate enough to be able to take time out from working, and for a while, I was a lady of leisure, jogging in the sunshine and shopping with my friends. My children had started school, so it was convenient and also enjoyable for me to focus on them as a stay-at-home mum. I loved picking them up from school, hearing their stories, jumping together on trampolines and getting creative with pasta pictures and toilet roll towers. One of my favourite times was designing bags with my children, because it reminded me of similar memories with my grandmother.

My daughter, Eleanor, designed a mermaid bag that was a beautiful sea blue colour covered with sparkling star netting that shimmered as it moved. William, however, wanted an army-style bag that was both stylish and practical. He chose a khaki camouflage material and designed pockets for his essentials, such as pen and paper to be ever ready, a torch for emergencies, a scarf for when you need a disguise, and of course a secret pocket for a snack on his adventures.

It was a truly wonderful time but I felt as if I needed my own mental stimulation with something to stretch and challenge me. I felt terribly guilty that being a full-time mum wasn't totally satisfying. I loved being with my children and doing creative things together, but I wanted some individuality back, to be my own person and not be just a mother or a wife.

As I was standing outside a Marks & Spencer shop one morning, waiting for my friend to arrive, I spotted a sign on their window saying they were looking for a visual merchandiser. "What's that?" I thought. I'd never heard of it before, and, seeing as I had time on my hands, I thought I'd pop in and find out about it; not that I was interested in the job – I was just curious to hear what it was. I know it might sound like a weird thing to do, but when I think about it now, it's the kind of random thing my father would probably do as well. Just ask a question and see where it gets you. Take action and think later.

One of the shop assistants greeted me as I entered the store, so I asked her about visual merchandising or 'VM' as she corrected me. She told me that it was styling the store and that I should come back the next day when the VM manager was available. She also told me to bring a C.V., which I thought was odd when I was just going for a chat and passing time.

The next day I decided to go back to the store because I was bored and curious. I'd always enjoyed meeting new people and it would be an interesting way of passing a few hours. What was the worst that could happen? I was about to find out.

I met Lovely Laura, the VM manager, who was smartly dressed in her uniform, with long dark hair and a calming voice. She made me feel at ease – not that I was particularly nervous – but some people just make you feel comfortable. They're the type of people you could sit and chat to all day.

I had an exciting morning with Lovely Laura and it was great fun. Firstly, she asked me to greet a customer as they came through the front door. Why would she want me to do that? That's odd, right? I'd just come for a chat. Nevertheless, I walked straight over to a customer, introduced myself and asked if they needed any help. That was easy.

After that, she showed me around the store asking me questions about the styling of the displays. I used my knowledge from dressmaking and my interior design course to answer her questions, telling her about the colour, style and composition of the arrangements. She looked surprised by how much I knew. That was fun, so what next?

Next was a trip up to the office where there was a rail of clothes. 'Interesting,' I thought. She asked me to put three outfits together for different ages of men. It was my kind of morning with something different and creative. I enjoyed the challenge.

When my husband came home from work, I couldn't wait to tell him about my day and how interesting it had been. Like every day, when he walked into the house, he asked if I had any news. Yes, today I got offered a job, and I didn't want a job. He was stunned, but not as much as I was when Laura offered me the position as a 'VM'. Was that day an opportunity waiting to happen or was it a crazy moment that I turned into reality? Whatever it was I had to decide what to do – whether to take the VM role or let it pass me by.

Well, as the saying goes 'in for a penny and in for a pound', so I decided to try it out on a part-time basis so that I could still pick up my children from school. It would give me a focus, teach me new skills, and, from what I'd experienced so far, it looked interesting and exciting. It would provide me with the independence to stretch my mind but also give me time with my children to create a nurturing family. It was a good compromise between life and work.

In my black ant-like uniform of stretchy trousers and long-line top, I was raring to go, feeling anxious but excited. I had a black bum bag with lots of pockets, like William's, filled with my essentials: such as pen and paper to be ever ready, a craft knife for emergencies, a pair of scissors that were always handy, and a secret pocket for my phone and chewing gum that would be confiscated if found.

Initially, I was responsible for styling the Women's Department. It became one of my favourite departments because it changed constantly and I was creating stories with my styling. I was reminded of the beautiful images from Vogue magazines that I coveted when I was a teenager. I loved the glamour. It gave me instant gratification and boosted my confidence.

After a few months I was moved around the departments, from the strength of the Men's to the softness of Lingerie and the fun of the Kids' departments. They all had their individual quirks, which were interesting to begin with, but I craved something more. I needed freedom to express myself. Working for a large company, there was only so much I could do outside of the guidelines. It felt restrictive, so what was I going to do next?

I thought I'd have a moment on television. Are you surprised? It was another opportunity that just came along. I can't remember where I saw the advert initially, but it was before social media so it was probably in a newspaper, and it was asking for people to enter into an interior design TV show – House Doctor. I didn't know what a House Doctor was but it sounded exciting. Here we go again; there was a theme to my actions.

There were live auditions one Saturday in London and, when I arrived, the queue was so massive that it snaked around several large office blocks, and I was waiting for hours. Luckily, it was a sunny day and eventually I was invited into a large room full of creative types. You know who I mean because they have wild hair, striking makeup and clothes that they've crafted themselves. I blended in perfectly.

I wasn't a jeans and t-shirt type of girl. I was adventurous and not embarrassed to express myself. I found my individuality when I was 16, which, as I write this, is a lightbulb moment. Maybe the loss of my grandmother gave me a boost to express my inner voice through my creative fashion style.

The waiting room was a bustle of noise with expressive gestures from flamboyant hopefuls. There was one girl in particular with tousled blonde hair and cheeks you just wanted to squeeze. She had a big personality, being loud and brash, so she got through the television auditions and onto the show.

When it came to my turn for the interview, I suddenly felt very nervous because I wasn't used to speaking in front of a camera. With my heart pounding, I struggled to answer the questions but the kind researcher said that I was a natural for TV. Of course she said that to everyone but I left feeling happy. I didn't get a call back, but it sparked my interest to find out more about the programme.

I discovered that the House Doctor programme was about the art of styling property for sale, because a more attractive property would ultimately increase the sale value and help it sell quicker. It was a new concept in the UK, brought over from America by celebrity interior designer Ann Maurice. I discovered that she taught workshops in London so I decided to dive in and join. It would complement my interior design studies and the workshops sounded exciting, so of course I was smitten. It was the course I needed to discover to piece my journey together.

The next few months provided the creative boost I was looking for, giving me the confidence to feel competent and successful in something once again, to feel the sense of reward and achievement, and to find my direction. After qualifying as a House Doctor consultant with Anne Maurice, I decided to take a step forwards, to leave my VM role with M&S and set up my own interior design practice. After qualifying in interior design, I'd already had some successful assignments with clients, so now was the time for me to take a leap of faith and focus on my new career.

I was on a path to something new and exciting, the creative spark that I'd been searching for. It would become my journey towards my own memories to cherish, a journey that would help me through my grief and make a difference to others. It would be a journey that would honour my father with new insights and values, creating memories not just for me but also for others to share.

I felt anxious and scared because it was a stretch beyond anything I'd known before and it all came about so unexpectedly. But, sometimes, to find your way, you have to firstly become lost. You have to be at a point of exhaustion so that your inner voice can surface, so that you're open to opportunities no matter how random they might appear, and you have to feel on the edge so that you're not scared if you fall and it all goes wrong.

With a sense of openness comes a richness of possibilities and with a feeling of bravery comes confidence. I couldn't be afraid because I was dreaming with my eyes wide open. It was a fabulous adventure just waiting to happen.

THE NEXT ADVENTURE

I began my interior design practice, GA Interiors, very slowly, trying out different projects to test the water, whilst making sure I was able to collect my children from school every day. Some of my favourite designs and experiences are the ones shared with you in this book. They're at the heart of the home and reflect on how all of my adventures have brought me to this point of connectivity – creating a stylish home with a healthy and happy space.

By the time I've finished writing this book, my son William will be at university and I'll be an empty nester. I don't like that phrase because the word *empty* sounds as if my life will become vacant and hollow. Maybe I am worried that my life will be empty without him close by me. I'm certainly going to miss the thudding of the football being kicked against the house, the constant opening of the fridge door with the rustling of packets, and the acrobatic bounces as he flies down the stairs like a missile on a mission.

Part of the emptiness will be not having him close by me every day, connecting me to my father; the bond between them so strong and his love ever present. When he surprises me with a cup of tea because he knows I'm feeling sad, just like my father. When he sits and softly tells me about his creative ideas, just like my father. When I watch him playing sports with the joy of bouncing a ball, just like my father.

Unlike my sisters who had to deal with the gravity of my father's loss many years ago, being with my son has given me comfort every day. From the moment my father took his last breath, I've hugged my son, embracing the love of them both.

I've felt blessed for 18 years to have him close beside me. When I look up, I see him there. I reach out and feel his love. I listen to hear his Northern twang. Now that William's leaving the family home, I feel the grief well up inside me and a sense of loss surrounds me. He's going and I'm frightened of losing him. I know these feelings are just my insecurities and part of the grief process that I have to finalise.

Although the grief shark is biting at my heels, this time I'm more prepared. Even though I feel apprehensive, sad and unsettled, I appreciate that it's just part of my journey. I don't feel empty or abandoned because I now have an encyclopaedia of memories to cherish.

Over the years I've nurtured my son William to be strong and independent, able to make decisions that keep him safe and secure. Although my heart breaks at not being able to hold him every day, I'm so proud of what he's achieved. I know he'll be amazing and I'm confident he'll be back for my Sunday roast.

As I take the next step forwards and launch this book as a tribute to my father, I feel confident that my creativity will blossom, giving me closure from the grief and sadness. Although my father is no longer present and my son has gone to university, they will forever be in my heart. Their memories will bring me joy and happiness every day.

The next adventure begins.

CHAPTER 1

GROWING UP

As an interior designer, I've become intrigued with the connectivity between interior style and health. I've found it interesting how an environment, in particular our homes, can affect our thoughts, feelings and actions, both positively and negatively. Don't you think it's fascinating how a simple change, like a refreshing paint colour, can make a space look attractive whilst at the same time create feelings of happiness and emotional wellbeing.

On the flip side, if you think that your home doesn't look attractive, then it could leave you feeling ashamed or embarrassed. Children and many adults are immensely vulnerable and impressionable, particularly now that we have social media showcasing everything as beautiful and gorgeous.

As you mature and grow out of your space, the décor becomes dated. I've seen this lead to feelings of anxiety, unhappiness, lack of sleep and even isolation. The easiest way for me to explain this connectivity between interior style and health is to share Skye's story with you.

I first met Skye's mother at a ladies' event, where she asked if I would help redesign her shower room because it was dated and she didn't know where to start. One day, whilst we were reviewing the project together, she mentioned how tired she was because her daughter was having trouble sleeping. Skye hadn't been sleeping well for some time so her mother was worried. She explained how lack of sleep was making Skye feel lethargic and unhappy, so she was finding it difficult to focus and concentrate at school. Not only was Skye stirring in the middle of the night, she was also waking her mother for comfort. The whole family was exhausted.

I know from personal experience with my own children that being a parent is hard enough, but when your child has difficulty sleeping then you'll do anything to get a good night's rest. So, I offered to take a look at Skye's bedroom to see if there was anything I could recommend, from a practical perspective, that would help Skye sleep and give her mother a rest.

When I first met Skye she was 11 years old and had just started secondary school. She was a pretty girl, softly spoken and shy. Her mother told me that she had friends at school but didn't invite them home and especially not for a sleepover. Skye explained that she was embarrassed by her bedroom and it was making her feel anxious. As the Journal of Sleep Research (*Review Paper 28Nov2017*) suggests, sleep disturbance is prevalent in children with anxiety.

For a girl so young to say that she felt anxious made me worry. Her feelings were starting to lead to physical symptoms such as stress, unhappiness and, of course, a lack of sleep with subsequent tiredness. It was affecting her ability to concentrate and achieve her full potential at school. My main concern, however, was that she was beginning to display signs of isolation by not having her friends over to enjoy time together.

Although it was simple to appreciate that Skye was having difficulty sleeping, it wasn't easy for her parents to see that the bedroom was the cause of their daughter's anxiety. As Skye showed me to her bedroom, all of her concerns came to light. I wasn't shocked by her room because it was a stereotypical girl's bedroom of pink and purple décor that looked dated and tired, but for Skye it had gone past the point of being comfortably shabby and moved into the realms of teenage trauma. It needed more than a lick of paint to help Skye feel organised, contented and proud of her room. It needed a complete design overhaul. From the furniture layout to storage solutions, from the colour scheme to lighting choice, and from the organisation to accessory styling, everything needed refreshing and modernising to look fabulous and to support Skye's physical growth and mental development. It needed to be practical and functional as well as absolutely gorgeous.

The size of the room was amazing, with a high ceiling and grand period features, but, like Skye, it was looking a little tired. In a corner of her bedroom, a stack of well-worn school books littered the carpet and a window the size of a giant's door flooded sunshine into the room. It was enlightening to see crazy photo booth snaps of her and her friends bejewelled on the walls.

Skye disliked the childish pink and purple décor because it no longer reflected her personality. She wanted her bedroom to be blue like the sky, which is why she chose the pseudonym of Skye for this story.

She was getting backache from crouching on her bed because she had nowhere to sit comfortably to do her homework, and was finding it difficult to focus properly on her studies. Skye explained that getting to sleep was difficult because, being tiny, her giant curtains were hard to close so she always had them half open and half closed, letting in light when she needed it to be dark and relaxing. But the problems didn't stop there in Skye's bedroom as her drawers were broken, her wardrobe was too small and she didn't have any shelves where she could store the library of books that she loved to read.

As Skye perched on the edge of the bed next to me, with her shoulders hunched, her head downcast and her voice trembling with despair, she shared how these problems were making her feel helpless because they were stopping her from tidying up and organising her room how she wanted. It made me sad hearing this because she was obviously keen and eager to tidy up. She had the enthusiasm but her storage was damaged, making her feel frustrated. Her room looked tired and cluttered but she wanted it to be organised and cosy.

You might ask why Skye's parents hadn't decorated the bedroom before it got to this stage, but life happens and sometimes you can't see the problem when you live with it. It's even more difficult to look at your home objectively when you're completely exhausted after being continuously woken every night. For Skye and her parents, like many struggling with dated décor, the problem is knowing where to start. With Skye's bedroom, there were many issues to address. It wasn't just a simple change; it needed a complete design overhaul as Skye was no longer a little girl.

I could hear Skye's anxiety and feel her pain as she explained how she'd grown out of the childish room style that was making her feel anxious and disturbing her sleep. She needed a boost of ideas in her bedroom to help nurture her growth and, of course, to help her sleep.

To understand Skye's concerns, I reviewed the emotional aspects of the bedroom decor:

HOW DID THE SPACE MAKE SKYE FEEL?	HOW DID SKYE WANT IT TO FEEL?
Anxious (Room looks childish)	Stylish (Mature room design)
Embarrassed (Broken cupboards)	Proud (Trendy furniture)
Dated (Pink and Purple decor)	Modern (Blue colour scheme)
Messy (Inadequate storage)	Tidy (Organised storage)
Lack of Sleep (Curtains don't close properly)	Restful (Curtains easy to close)
Painful Backache (No desk)	Energising (Desk for studying)

Skye wanted her bedroom to feel calming, practical and sociable. She wanted it to be fun and lively, a space to enjoy with friends. Reviewing each of these words made it easier to identify the changes needed to create her perfect bedroom.

To help her feel calm, I introduced a clean, crisp colour scheme of blue and white. Blue was chosen by Skye because it reminded her of happy holidays at the seaside. It's also a cool, calming colour that's relaxing for the mind and body because it can help lower blood pressure and reduce a rapid heart rate. It was the ideal colour choice to help balance Skye's anxiety.

Rather than having plain painted blue walls, I decided to give the bedroom a design boost by introducing wallpaper with a modern floral style – my field of dreams. I felt nervous showing Skye my 'field of dreams' design because I wanted to get it right and for her to be overjoyed. Having children myself, I know that kids can be totally honest, so if she didn't like it then she would tell me immediately.

It wasn't just wallpaper of blue and white flowers that I chose because I'd decided on the 'field of dreams' design to help Skye feel surrounded by nature. I wanted the flowers to ramble over the main bedroom wall so that Skye would see them from her bed. When she went to sleep, the soothing pattern would help her feel calm and relaxed. Then, in the morning, it would help her to feel invigorated, as if she'd woken up in a field of flowers. What you see first thing in the morning influences your day and will either help you wake up feeling energised or deflated. What do you see in the morning?

My heart was beating rapidly as I showed Skye my new design for her bedroom. She was quiet for a moment, with her head downcast. This made me think, 'How on earth could I have got it so wrong?' I felt as if she didn't even want to talk to me because she couldn't find the words to express her dislike. I felt absolutely awful because I wanted her to feel inspired, and I wanted her to love the new design with all her heart. Now I was the one feeling anxious, searching Skye's face for any clue as to how she felt about my 'field of dreams' design.

With tears in her eyes, she slowly looked up at me and said, "This is the dream that was in my head." My heart burst with joy. I was so relieved to have created her childhood dream. Even today, I can recollect the happiness in her eyes and her smile wide with excitement.

As I looked over at Skye's mother, I sensed her worry release as she hugged her daughter. The joy between them was heart-warming and there was a sense of hope that the new design would help Skye to feel positive and relaxed, and to get a good night's sleep.

To create a healthy and invigorating bedroom for Skye, I designed the room to be multi-purpose with clearly-defined areas for work (desk), rest (bed) and play (beanbag). To control the amount of light in her bedroom, I replaced the curtains at her giant window with a roman blind and an easy to reach metal chain pulley. It was a small change but an important one, because she could now alter the light in her bedroom, enabling her to control the mood and aid a restful night's sleep. It's important for any design solution not only to look good but to be appropriate for the age and mobility of the person using the space. A healthy environment enables you to move around and use the space effectively with maximum ease and minimum effort.

Another vital change needed in Skye's bedroom was the removal of the fitted wardrobe because it was too small and badly organised for her possessions. It was making her feel anxious because she couldn't organise her belongings and put them away how she wanted. I replaced the fitted wardrobe and broken drawers with a large, free-standing wardrobe. With hanging space as well as internal shelves and drawers, it instantly improved the organisation of her clothes, shoes and accessories. Having one large unit instead of several smaller, broken and ill-fitting units freed up space in her bedroom for a desk and her chill-out area.

Her chill-out area was the sociable space that she longed for, to share with her friends. Next to her comfy beanbag was a new shelving unit adorned with Skye's mementos from her childhood, treasures from holidays, cheeky snaps of her friends and her beloved books. Having things in the bedroom connecting to happy memories created positive energy that helped to invigorate Skye every day.

A desk was crucial to Skye's new bedroom because it meant that she didn't have to slouch on her bed to complete her homework. It would give her the correct posture she needed to work effectively, and it was satisfying to hear that her school grades improved as a direct consequence. She no longer had back-ache and could achieve her full potential when studying. The desk also doubled as a dressing table for applying makeup and styling her hair before parties with friends. She was growing up quickly.

When you're living in one room with limited space, it's important for furniture to have dual functionality. There are many options on the high street such as a bed with integrated storage, a coffee table which can transform into a dining table, and a wardrobe which incorporates a full-length mirror. The smaller the room, or the more activities you're trying to accommodate in one space, the more detailed the design needs to be to make sure it's functional and practical as well as stylish. When a space suits your lifestyle and the way you like to live, then it becomes a healthy and nurturing environment.

As we headed to the shops to buy the furniture and accessories, Skye and her mother were very excited. It was such fun because Skye was so enthusiastic. Her face was splashed with a constant smile as she bounced happily around the stores.

Skye's new bedroom was no longer a teenage trauma because it had become a safe, sensory and stylish space. Focusing on the emotional elements of Skye's anxiety helped to create a bedroom for her that not only looked fantastic, but, most importantly, also felt amazing. Her bedroom became a nurturing sleep sanctuary and a happy space that she could joyfully share with her friends.

My final day with Skye was in her bedroom, creating a floral notice board that would sit above her new desk, providing space to display all of her photos with friends. She was exhilarated to see it all coming together, especially when two of her friends called over. She showed them straight into her bedroom beaming with pride.

Her friends were literally jumping with delight, swivelling up and down on her desk chair, sinking into her chill-out bean bag and collapsing on her bed together in fits of giggles. It was time for me to leave.

Since the makeover, I've seen Skye's mother looking refreshed and smiling with delight, saying that her daughter is now sleeping soundly. Her concentration has improved and her school grades have increased. She enjoys having her friends over to stay and doesn't want to come out of her bedroom because it's relaxing and comfortable.

This experience taught me that it's important for personal space to change and evolve as we grow. Even as adults, our lives are continuously changing so it's essential to refresh our space and create a healthy environment. As can be seen from Skye's story, an unhealthy space can lead to physical problems (lack of sleep and tiredness) as well as emotional issues (anxiety and unhappiness).

From Skye's story, it's also important to recognise how an unhealthy space can affect a child's early development. From the moment a child is born, they are being stimulated by their environment. An unhealthy space can be detrimental, restricting growth and progress whilst a healthy and nurturing space will facilitate a child to achieve their best. Skye is now blissfully happy with her peaceful, relaxing and organised space that she enjoys with her friends, creating memories that she will cherish forever.

WHERE TO START WITH INTERIOR DESIGN

When you've lived in a space for several years, it can be difficult to see how to change and refresh it. It becomes normal and you get used to the problems, so you put up with things that are less than perfect, like a cupboard handle that's been missing for years and you only decide to put it back when you're selling your home or have guests to stay. All those years of trying to pinch the cupboard door to prise it open and now that it's fixed, you have a handle that feels like a luxury. Why didn't you do it before and why is it only now that you make the effort to fix it? Things are usually left because the problem either wasn't a nuisance before or you didn't actually see the problem.

Even when you've moved into a new house, the root of the problem or areas for improvement can be difficult to recognise because you have no history with the property. So, where do you start when modernising a space?

Most people begin a makeover by focusing on things, such as: I need a new sofa, a pair of curtains or a ceiling light. This is how you create a stylish home, but it doesn't necessarily mean that it will be healthy.

Is it more important to have style over substance or substance over style in your interior space? I recommend that it's important to balance both.

If you have a chair that's stylish then it can make you feel proud and rewarded every time you look at it. It can showcase your design flair and creativity, it can symbolise the hard work you've put in to achieve it and it often represents your heritage or personal taste. But, if that chair is uncomfortable to sit on then it's pushed to a corner of the room, looking good but totally useless. You're disappointed.

If you have a chair that's lost its looks but is so comfortable that you don't want to get rid of it, then it will divide your emotions. Your head is telling you to buy something new, but your heart can't let go. I was once in a conversation with a woman who was in such a predicament. Her sofa was propped up on a stack of hardback books after the legs had given way, and the seat was scattered with cushions to make it feel comfortable where it sagged in the middle. But, she wasn't ready to get rid of it because it was the sofa where she'd spent precious time nurturing her children. Although she had fond memories tied up in the sofa, it was no longer stylish and had become unhealthy because it was giving her backache and causing her pain. It was comforting her emotionally, but not physically.

If you take a moment to think about your favourite chair, how does it make you feel? It might be a chaise longue that's relaxing and helps you to think clearly. It might be an office swivel chair that keeps you focused and energised to work at your optimum. It might be a sprawling sofa for the family to cosy up on at the end of a long day. It could even be a garden bench where you've created a sanctuary to escape from the busyness of life. Your favourite chair is not just an object to sit on because it has your feelings and emotions attached to it. It creates a moment of excitement, pleasure and happiness.

My favourite chair is a long, modern, leather sofa in my garden room. It's comfortable, not just for me but also when the kids come and snuggle up beside me to share their thoughts of the day. Sitting in a chair that has a place for others to join me invites them to share my space. It encourages affection with cuddles and promotes conversation with its relaxing, informal setting. My sofa is stylish but it's my favourite chair because it creates a healthy environment for me to share love and affection with my family.

When any interior makeover, I recommend that you focus on style and substance. The way to do this is by reflecting on emotions and then correlating them into style.

The majority of rooms are multi-function spaces that are segmented into different areas. For a healthy and stylish home, you need to understand how you use each area and, subsequently, how you want it to feel. For example, you might relax in the sitting room and want it to feel cosy; enjoy a coffee with friends in the kitchen and want it to feel welcoming; soak away your troubles in the bathroom and want it to feel relaxing; or sleep in the bedroom to find a moment of peace and quiet.

As adults, we generally spend 90% of our time in an environment. If we frequently vary our space to change our mood, then it's an ideal way of feeling positive and staying healthy, but, what about teenagers who are renowned for hibernating in their bedroom and only surfacing for pizza? How do they change their surroundings to stay energised and positive?

Maybe you're in a situation where you've had to downsize and you're now feeling squashed into a smaller space? This happened to my friend who parted from her husband after 20 years marriage and then moved into a rented room. Her bedroom was also her office and the living space. She wanted it to feel spacious, a haven and a sanctuary, but it felt small, cramped and overwhelming.

A multi-function room will have different emotions attached to each area depending on who is using the space and the time of day. For example, my living room will be invigorating in the morning to wake me up, peaceful in the afternoon when I'm taking a break from designing and need a moment to think, and then soothing in the evening when it's time to kick back and relax.

It was interesting to see how flexible my living room was when I had a large family party that was supposed to be in the garden but ended up indoors thanks to the unpredictability of the British weather. In the early part of the evening, my living room was a peaceful space for the older and quieter members of my family. As the evening wore on, it was taken over by the teenage boys to watch an important football game, before it was commandeered by my lively *Prosecco* friends.

Each group had their own requirements: the oldies wanted to shut the door for peace and quiet to have time to chat with family members they hadn't seen in a while, the kids wanted to shut the door so they could concentrate on watching the game and share football commentary, whilst my *Prosecco* friends wanted to shut the door so that they could let their hair down and the kids couldn't see their party antics. Each time I went into the living room, there was a totally different vibe and energy in the space. I designed my living room to be stylish, but also relaxing and cosy so that it would feel comfortable for my friends and family. When a room feels comfortable, it encourages inclusion and conversation.

To create a room that's comfortable, it's important to understand how you want to use the space. What are the activities in the space? A bedroom is often sleeping + reading + dressing, whereas a living room might be sitting with friends + playing with the children + watching television. If you jot down your list of activities on the *Your Memories*

To Cherish page, you can refer back to it later when piecing together your design.

Once you have your list of activities, then you can start to analyse how your space feels for each activity. You're starting to look at the connection between interiors and emotions, to create your home of wellness. Maybe you'd like your space to feel calm and relaxing, energising and uplifting, organised and practical, light and spacious, fun and characterful or even chic and trendy. What words would you use to describe how you want your space to feel? It's always one of the first questions I ask when I'm designing a room. Begin by writing down how your space feels at the moment and then list how you would like it to feel. You only need to write down a couple of key words and, if you can't think of your own words, here are some of the most frequent ones my clients use:

HOW DOES YOUR SPACE FEEL?	HOW DO YOU WANT YOUR SPACE TO FEEL?
Dark	Light
Dated	Modern
Bland	Warm & Welcoming
Cluttered	Organised
Crowded	Spacious

You then take these key words into your design to create an interior that looks great and feels fantastic. For example, my living room is cosy, relaxing and sociable, whereas my garden room is spacious, light and family-friendly. Both rooms are modern and have been published in national interior design magazines, but they have a different look and feel. I designed the living room with soft textures, velvet sofas and a luxurious carpet to maximise slow, relaxing energy. I designed the garden room with glossy textures, leather sofas and ceramic floor tiles to encourage invigorating and lively energy. The garden room is ideal as a party space whereas the living room is the after-party chill-out hideaway.

Focusing on how a room will feel ensures the balance of texture, colour and style all come together to create your ideal space that's cohesive, healthy and stylish.

The words you choose that describe how it feels at the moment are from your consciousness. They help you identify problems with your space. You can see that your space is dark, cluttered or bland. But, the words that you choose to describe how you want it to feel come from your subconscious emotion. You want it to feel spacious, organised or warm and welcoming. Your emotions help you identify potential solutions. If your space is dark and you want it to feel brighter, your focus is on improving the light. If it's cluttered and you want it to feel organised, your focus is on storage. If it's bland and you want it to feel warm and welcoming, your focus is to find a colour that you love to add energy to the space.

The key words will also keep you focused and help to save you time when you go shopping. If you want a modern look and spacious feel then you can discard traditional or bulky furniture. If you want cool blue colours then you can walk past the shelf of fiery red accessories. Creating a successful design for your interior space focuses on continual elimination until you piece together a design that blends style and emotions. It looks good and feels right.

In summary, when deciding where to start, make a list of the activities in your space, then jot down a couple of words to describe how it feels at the moment and how you want it to feel. You can then feed these words into your design and use them when sourcing products to create your dream home.

YOUR MEMORIES TO CHERISH

This is your personal space to record the memories you never want to forget. Take a moment to jot down, draw or scribble your thoughts and ideas...

CHAPTER 2

SECOND CHILD SYNDROME

It was a bright summer's day when I received a phone call from an anxious mother, distressed about her baby boy. Like me, she had an older daughter but it was her 18-month-old son who was having trouble sleeping. Up until that point he'd been a good sleeper, but since he'd learnt to walk, he no longer wanted to sleep in his own bedroom.

Adele, his mother, woefully described how each night her son, Jamie, would start off sleeping in his cot and then, in the dark of the night, he would go into stealth mode and escape. I don't know if you've ever seen videos of escaping toddlers, but when a child wants to get out of a cot, they can be very determined and resourceful. Adele never saw Jamie clambering over the bars of his cot, secretly tiptoeing out of his bedroom and sliding into his sister's bed each night. But, that's where she'd find him each morning.

I remember when my own son was a toddler and used to sneak into my bed in the middle of the night. He would climb up onto my bed and then clamber over me so that he was nestled in the middle. As he woke me each night, I'd pick him up and carry him back to his own bed. Cleverly, he became adept at sliding in beside me without disturbing my sleep. I'd wake in the morning to feel his head on my shoulder and arm slung around my neck for mummy cuddles.

Every morning, Adele would find Jamie nestled next to his four-year-old sister, Lottie, with their arms intertwined. It sounded idyllic, and a blessing that the two children wanted to be with each other, but Adele was concerned that Jamie was becoming over-dependant on his sister.

When Adele asked me to review Jamie's bedroom, she knew that it was bland and uninspiring, but she didn't know how to decorate the room so that it would entice Jamie to sleep in his own bed. She knew something had to be done but she was lost for ideas and didn't want to make any expensive mistakes.

When Adele talked to me about Lottie's bedroom, she was animated and excited. Her words were full of colour and delight. However, when she mentioned Jamie's bedroom her shoulders were hunched and it was obvious to see how she was physically exasperated.

She wanted Jamie to sleep in his own bed. Not only was she hoping that he would feel more comfortable and relaxed in his own room, but it would also give Lottie the opportunity to have an improved night's sleep. As well as creating a relaxing and calming bedroom for Jamie, Adele was hoping that the makeover would also create an exciting and independent play space for him. It would give him the confidence to learn on his own and not be reliant on his sister for company or motivation.

Adele firstly showed me into Lottie's bedroom. As I stepped into the room, it was late in the afternoon and the two young children were like peas in a pod. Under the covers of the bed, with their bodies stapled together, two smiling faces beamed out at me over the book they were reading. The two little munchkins politely said, "Hello".

As I looked around the room, it was a riot of colour and excitement. The walls were swathed in soft, sugary pink with white billowing 'cloud like' curtains framing the window. Beside the window was a mini library with a rainbow of books, nestled on a soft fluffy rug next to a bubble gum pink beanbag. I noticed how the beanbag was gently hollowed and could imagine the daughter enjoying a moment of adventure, transported into another world with a story. It reminded me of how my own daughter loved to read and would sleep with books hidden in her bed like a fond friend.

In a corner of Lottie's bedroom was a fantasy of frill: a rail of Disney princess dresses lined up neatly waiting for the show to begin. Matching glitter plastic shoes lined up beneath them in anticipation of a dance. Lottie loved to dance, her imagination flowing with every step. Lottie's bedroom was an explosion of colour, texture and fun.

After the excitement of Lottie's room, Adele showed me into Jamie's bedroom. By contrast it was completely bland. It felt cold and sad, so it was no surprise that Jamie always rushed into Lottie's den of entertainment.

Jamie's bedroom walls were painted showroom magnolia, plain and uninteresting. Although it's a popular colour for selling houses, it's also dreary and devoid of personality. In the centre of the room was Jamie's cot, a modern circular style, painted cream and complemented with a cream waffle baby blanket. The only other item in the room was a large, cream modern wardrobe, faced with a full-length mirror reflecting the contemporary curves of the cot. There were no toys, no books and nothing to stimulate Jamie's interest. It was as if he'd been given a piece of bread and his sister was indulging in chocolate cake.

The room had Second Child Syndrome. This is where the bedroom of the first child was colourful and exciting but, the décor of the second child was almost forgotten. It looked as if the parents hadn't bothered to welcome Jamie into the home. They placed the bare necessities in the spare room and called it Jamie's bedroom, but there was no emotional connection or personality added to the space. It wasn't because they didn't care about or love their second child. It usually happens because decorating the bedroom of the first child was a novelty, but, by the time the second child is born, the parents are frequently exhausted with less time, energy and enthusiasm.

Jamie didn't want to play or sleep in the uninspiring room and he'd found a way of breaking free. He wanted to be in Lottie's bedroom with the bright colours, amazing toys and tantalising textures. It was far more exciting.

Jamie was too young to express his own ideas, so I discussed his needs with Adele and also watched him as he played. When designing Jamie's new bedroom, I considered his age, physicality and personality. Whether it's a child or an adult, these three things are key factors to any good interior design. What age are they now and how long does the design need to last before the next stage of development? What physical capabilities do they have and are there any special requirements? What interests them and how can that be incorporated into the design?

With such a young child, it can often be tempting to choose stereotypical gender styles of pink and fluffy for girls, with blue cars or trains for boys. It certainly worked for Lottie, but Jamie was an adventurer so I wanted to create a design that was more individual for him, with an action-packed bedroom to explore. I wanted to create niches of joy and excitement, a room that would take Jamie far away from the bland, to nurture his development whilst fuelling his imagination.

By the time a child reaches the age of two, their character is starting to evolve. Around the same time, they enjoy make-believe play so an engaging bedroom can help to stimulate their senses, build their skills and develop their personality. Jamie had reached the next stage of development, an age where he was active and inquisitive. He loved to climb. As I watched Jamie play with Lego and Play-Doh, building creations from his imagination, it helped me to understand his interests. I could appreciate his personality as he thwarted a dragon (actually a soft toy rabbit), so that his sister Lottie would be saved from peril (the plastic shoes were pinching her and she wanted to kick them off).

I replaced the cot for a big boy cabin bed with a den and a slide that would provide an ideal play area to expand his imagination and develop his personality. The slide would be his escape route; great fun and far safer than climbing over cot railings. Even if he did leave his bed in the middle of the night, he'd be back up for another slide until he wore himself out and finally settled to sleep.

Hidden beneath the bed was a den, screened off by a curtain and painted with a woodland scene, where he could pretend to be camping in a faraway forest, the king of a castle or sailing away in a boat on his next adventure. It was his own private den where he could hide and feel secure, lounging amongst the soft colourful cushions.

Along one wall, a shelf unit was neatly organised with treasure boxes. Each box was painted with an image and words to show the toys hiding within. It was easy for him to see where everything was and also a simple learning exercise to help him tidy up.

Next to the den was a trundle truck with his favourite books. He could wheel them into his den or take them into Lottie's bedroom to stock up his library. His favourite activity was to hide the books in his den and then get Lottie to wheel him around the bedroom making train noises.

It was now a room for pure imagination. It would stimulate

Jamie's learning during the day by providing an exciting space encouraging him to laugh and play, and create a safe and secure place for him to relax and sleep soundly.

I was overjoyed when Adele phoned me to say that Jamie was happily playing in his own room and sleeping the whole night in his own bed. The only problem now was that Lottie wanted her bedroom redecorated!

FUTURE-PROOF DESIGN

Decorating rooms can be costly, time-consuming, disruptive and exhausting, so we're usually averse to changing them frequently. For this reason, rooms need to be future-proofed so that they will last until you're ready to refresh them. However, no interior design is completely future-proofed because, as we grow and develop, our needs change and alter – maybe you've bought your first house, moved in with your partner, got divorced, had a baby, become a grandparent, decided to get a dog or are suffering from an illness. With each change, your life alters and, subsequently, your home also needs to move on to help support and nurture you for each new circumstance.

Children's rooms, in particular, need refreshing the most, as they grow and develop dramatically in the early years. A baby's bedroom requires storage for many small items like nappies, creams, vests and bodysuits. A toddler's bedroom needs boxes that help organise toys, allowing sufficient space to run around. Between toddler and teenage years, a young child's bedroom requires plenty of floor space to be creative and expand their imagination. A teenage bedroom is a leap up towards adulthood, where exams and revision become more of a focus, so a desk for studying is needed next to shelves that organise school books. Every stage has its own specific requirements, so one room design isn't suitable for each stage of development.

You generally need to update a child's space (bedroom or playroom) every three to five years, but for an adult space (living room, master bedroom, office) you can often leave the décor much longer until it becomes dated or you have a major change of circumstances. For example, I decorated my daughter's bedroom when she was 16 so that it would inspire her through major years of examinations. She's now gone through that stage and enjoying university, so I won't redecorate her bedroom again until she's finished her degree. It will remain the same so that she feels comfortable in her room when she returns home for holidays. After she's finished her studies, if she then decides to move back home, we'll create a new bedroom design together, but if she prefers to live away from home then I'll turn it into a guest bedroom. The same décor won't last forever, so be mindful to prepare for the future and the next stage of life's adventure.

Understanding how long a design will last can help you to future-proof a room and apportion your budget appropriately. For example, if you're changing a child's bedroom within three years then you might choose inexpensive furniture. Whereas, a living room that's not going to be decorated for many years might incorporate more expensive furniture.

Once you've decided how long the interior décor needs to last, and how much money you want to spend on the makeover, you can then review the use of space in detail. To future-proof a room, whilst creating a healthy environment, the key considerations are that it is age appropriate, suits your physicality and reflects your personality.

AGE APPROPRIATE:

To create a space that lasts over time, a design needs to be age appropriate. It should incorporate the current stage of development, but also enhance growth or support decline.

If you're decorating a child's room, or you're at an age where you're going through a spate of changes in your life, then you might consider a flexible design that can change depending on your circumstances. One way of incorporating flexibility into your design is with furniture that alters as your needs change – a cot that turns into a bed, a desk that will also be used as a dressing table, a console table that expands to a dining table, or a sofa that converts into a bed. Varying the use of space helps to elongate the longevity of the design before it requires a complete makeover.

With many people living longer and looking to stay younger, it's sometimes brushed under the carpet that as we get older there are often more aches and pains that need to be considered, particularly when designing something as personal as a home. Rooms need to be designed for the downside as well as the upside of age. Those creaking bones might need an orthopaedic mattress, arthritis in the hands requires handles that are easy to grip, and a walking-frame is better suited to wood flooring.

When a room design is age appropriate, it creates a healthy environment that's practical as well as attractive. It makes the space feel comfortable and safe to move around in. It's also easier to tidy up because it's organised to suit the mobility and development stage of you and your family.

PHYSICALITY:

When style is the primary focus of a design, the emphasis is on how the room looks. However, when health and physicality sit alongside style, then the focus shifts to creating wellness.

Mobility is a key factor that's sometimes overlooked when designing a room – a child that runs around and needs rounded edges in case they bump into furniture, a gangly teenager who's accident prone and needs wipeable flooring for when they drop things, a wheelchair user who needs wide access to get about effortlessly, or a person who's not steady on their feet and needs soft flooring in case they fall. Mobility influences the furniture, flooring, storage and space planning requirements for interior designs.

As mobility changes, a design needs to be reviewed for adjustments. My mother suffered many years with arthritis, particularly in her hands and feet, and as the condition worsened she found it difficult to grip things; door knobs were challenging for her to turn and open but door handles were easier, enabling her to keep her independence and dignity. Being able to move about easily and safely is of vital importance for any interior.

Flooring choice is central to any design, but particular attention is needed with regards to mobility. Hard flooring, such as wood or tiles, allows ease of movement for wheelchairs, walking aids and children's toys. It doesn't, however, provide comfort if you're prone to falls. A short pile carpet is suitable if you're unsteady on your feet because it's a soft surface, for comfort and safety, that's easier to move about on. Carpet is also suitable for babies and younger children who play on the floor. It provides a comfy surface that feels warm and nurturing. There's been many a time I've appreciated a cosy carpet to stretch out on whilst constructing an endless complexity of Star Wars Lego with my son, William.

Whether you need walking aids or are able bodied, successful space planning is critical to create a healthy setting that meets your personal needs. When space planning, I recommend that you start by drawing the shape of your room and then add on your windows and doors. Next, draw in the walkways. It might be the route from one door to another door or from the door to the window. If you have walking aids or a wheelchair then the walkways would be wider to accommodate your individual needs and provide a safe layout. You can then start to incorporate furniture into the design so that it doesn't interfere with the walkways.

As well as mobility, another important consideration related to physicality is allergies. If your home is designed to keep you healthy, then it must allow for individual sensitivities. Maybe you have a dust allergy, pollen sensitivity or come out in a rash with certain fabrics. All of these need to be addressed in a design if it's to provide lasting health and wellness.

During the Victorian period, London's air was smog-filled, so voile blinds and heavy, draped curtains were layered and hung at windows to help reduce the amount of air pollution in the home. Today, we have a choice of blinds and curtains that help to block polluted air from entering the home, as well as natural air purifiers, such as plants, alongside air conditioning units that help improve air quality. But, as we take down walls for open-plan living and bi-fold doors, it's mindful to consider members of the family who suffer from pollen sensitivity. As an alternative, you could consider installing French glazed doors instead of expansive bi-fold doors, to reduce the amount of opening and potential air pollution.

Fabric sensitivity is particularly important when designing a bedroom because we all want to have a restful night's sleep. Sensitivity between the sheets can lead to a night of discomfort. Natural fabrics such as cotton, linen or silk have always been popular for bedding but bamboo is also taking a leap into the bedroom. If you're going through the menopause, suffer from overheating or sweat during the night, you could also consider moisture wicking or temperature regulating bedding. It's worth investing in the right type of bedding that makes you feel great because lack of sleep can lead to other problems such as lack of concentration, in addition to stress and anxiety.

If you suffer from dust allergies, a modern and contemporary style interior is most suitable because it incorporates clean lines with less fabric. But it doesn't have to look bland and you don't have to choose a sterile environment, getting rid of everything. Instead of choosing smaller accessories, opt for a big feature item such as a large vase that is easier to clean. Modern window treatments, such as simple Roman blinds or eyelet curtains, use less material and collect less dirt than more traditional styles, like festoon blinds or goblet headed curtains. To complete the room, a hard flooring is preferable to a carpet because it's easy to see the dust and quicker to clean it away. The modern style will create an attractive room without the fuss, making it easier for you to control dust and dirt, subsequently helping to reduce your risk of allergic reactions.

When health and physicality sit alongside style, they create lasting wellness.

PERSONALITY:

When designing a room, a little personality in your home will help you to connect with the space on an emotional level. It can help you to relax in the evening and invigorate you during the day.

Personality can be added to a room in several ways – through colour, pattern, furniture, style or accessories. In particular, the items that you have around you reflect your personality and can help you to feel calm or invigorated as you're reminded of the fond memories attached to them – the gold star award, swimming certificate, sports cup, running medal, letter from a friend or picture of our favourite place. They reflect you, the things you like to do and the relationships you cherish. When you look at the items, they nurture you with thoughts of achievement, friendships or affection.

One client in particular called me in to refresh his master bedroom. John was feeling anxious as he couldn't sleep and was finding it difficult to motivate himself to get out of bed each morning. His bedroom hadn't been decorated since he moved in and it was feeling cramped and crowded, not at all the restful space to call his sanctuary. The layout didn't suit his lifestyle, the décor was dated and the room wasn't reflecting his personality.

As I entered the bedroom, an oversized fitted wardrobe dominated the space and his bed was squashed into an alcove. There was no space to get in or out of bed comfortably, so rolling off the end was de rigueur. This is fun when you're a child but John wanted to be able to step out of bed like an adult. I recommended swapping the room over, with modern fitted wardrobes in the alcove and a luxurious master bed central to the room. When I showed John the design, he liked this idea because it would make the room feel spacious and less cramped whilst being modern and elegant.

The chintzy floral curtains and pastel green colour scheme didn't reflect John's personal style. With a new masculine colour scheme of blue and grey to modernise the room and an adult bed where he could get in and out with ease, it would be his perfect dream bedroom.

With the new layout, I designed fitted wardrobes, facing the bed, with two cupboards for clothes and open shelves in the middle, to display John's personal photos and treasures that he'd collected from his travels. This was an important space to place objects that would reflect his personality and inspire him. Before he went to sleep and when he woke up every morning, he could see all of the precious items. They would bring back positive and happy thoughts, helping him to relax peacefully to sleep and encourage him to wake feeling energised. Just a small touch of his personality in the room helped to reduce his anxiety. With improved sleep, he was back to his happy self.

In conclusion, to future proof your space, take into consideration all of your wellbeing needs when creating an interior design. Look at how you feel now and how you might feel in the immediate future. The immediate future is the length of time you can foresee that the design needs to last for you and your family.

When your home is personalised, it's unique to you and your lifestyle, creating a welcoming space that feels comfortable and helping you feel cherished.

YOUR MEMORIES TO CHERISH

This is your personal space to record the memories you never want to forget. You can take a moment to jot down, draw or scribble your thoughts and ideas.

CHAPTER 3

A NEW BEGINNING

One of my first assignments was thanks to Amy, another interior designer that I'd met through the House Doctor network. She was extremely generous and helpful, giving me opportunities to improve my skills and increase my confidence.

Although I didn't know much about the assignment, the adrenaline was pouring through my body and I was feeling hyper-excited as we headed towards north London in her Jeep. I was surprised that there was very little in her car apart from the two of us, a box with food for our lunch and several rolls of heavy duty recycling bags. I didn't really know what to expect but surely all interior design jobs included cushions? Where were they? Maybe she'd already delivered them to the property.

Amy said that we would be decluttering. 'Great!' I thought. I was good at organising so this would be a simple sort-out, rearrange a few shelves and plump some cushions to make it look pretty. Wow, was I in for a wake-up call.

As Amy parked the car, she pointed to an unassuming house at the end of a terrace. I was hit with reality as soon as the front door was opened, where a tiny lady with jet-black hair was waiting for us at the door. With her pale complexion, she stood to one side to let us in, but it was obvious that she didn't want to open the door wide, or rather, that she couldn't open the door wide due to the mound of oozing recycling bags blocking the hallway. As I clambered over the recycling bags, I thought she was having a clear-out. I hate to use the phrase 'tip of the iceberg,' but this was the start of things to come.

Amy showed me into the kitchen which I could appreciate was

very large but I couldn't actually see the space due to a huge mound of recycling bags stacked up against one wall. In my head, I calculated about 20 bags. What were they doing piled up in the kitchen and why had they overflowed into the hall? With her head bowed in embarrassment, the lady explained that these were bags of clothes waiting to be washed, but they weren't being washed because there was nowhere to hang them out to dry. I was shocked. I could see a washing line in the garden but you couldn't open the back door to reach it because of the clutter stacked in front of it. The layers of dust were so thick on the door handle that you could see it hadn't been opened for years.

All of the windows in the two-bedroom house were the same, with a multitude of things stacked up in front of them and a curtain of dust and grime blocking the path to fresh air. Subsequently, all of the rooms felt dark and musty, as if the life and energy had been sucked out of the house. In my naivety I wondered how the house could get like this. But, at least we were there to do something about it now, sort it out and fluff some cushions.

Amy asked me to focus on helping the 18-year-old daughter, Camille, whilst she assisted the mother. The daughter was polite, but she seemed anxious and embarrassed. She didn't want to look at me, but I could see the sadness in her eyes and the worry on her face.

We made our way upstairs to Camille's bedroom, where I struggled to enter because of the layers of stuff on her bedroom floor. It was a jumbled mess of texture and colour.

I began sorting out the stuff on the floor: headache tablets, a pair of jeans, headache tablets, a random shoe, headache tablets, a lonesome sock and headache tablets. I'd never seen someone with so many packets of headache tablets, so I found an empty shoe box and started to pop all of the packets within it. I was shocked and stunned to see the tablets overflowing the box, like a tsunami of pain. I had to take a moment, catch my breath and process what I was seeing. This was an 18-year-old girl who was 'getting by' with headache tablets to relieve physical pain, caused as a direct consequence of the stagnant and depressive air in her bedroom. I could understand how Camille's mother had called for help because the house had got to a point where it was making them physically, mentally and emotionally ill.

It made me feel so sad that Camille had been living like this, and it was a shocking realisation that's always stayed fresh in my mind.

The daughter's bedroom was so disorganised that it had got to a stage where tidying up was a huge effort, time consuming, stressful and a burden. How had it become so bad? As the daughter sat next to me, looking away, she recounted how miserable she felt because, "I've tried so hard to tidy up but feel as if I'm getting nowhere." She would diligently try to tidy up her bedroom, putting things away as best she could, but then she'd run out of time and have to go to college, leaving a mountain of mess behind her. Camille was tirelessly trying to create an organised bedroom but she just moved things around her room. She didn't know, and had never been taught, how to let go of things that were no longer useful, so she kept everything.

Her mother's bedroom was similar and it was worrying to see how unhealthy habits can so easily pass through generations.

Amy suggested that I should go through Camille's things with her so that I could teach her effective organisational skills, so we traipsed her bin bags of clothes into the living room where there was a little more space. As I held up each item, Camille had to say, "stay" or "go".

If it was stay then I hung the garment on a hanger to go into her wardrobe, and if it was go then I placed it into a labelled bag for recycling.

For some of the items she wanted to keep, I challenged her decisions to help develop her analytical skills. She had to think about what would be useful to her and what she could live without. Because she'd not been taught how to get rid of the shoe that no longer had a heel, the jeans that were too small and the top that had ripped beyond repair, she was seeking my permission to let them go.

At first, Camille was really keen and making decisions on what should go or stay. Then her mother came into the room and switched on the television to the gospel choir station. She became distracted as the two of them began to sing and sway to the music. I'd never watched anything like this before, but it was enlightening to see how the uplifting music and positive messages were giving them both strength and hope. They sang loudly and looked at each other fondly as they created a moment when they didn't have to worry about the mess.

It made my heart melt when Camille suddenly turned to look at me and said, with tears rolling down her face, "I've been praying for someone to come and help us clear the clutter. It was too much for us to do on our own and we didn't know where to start." With my eyes welling with tears, it was a moment of utter joy as I felt blessed to be able to help.

As I focused Camille back to sorting through the mound of clothes, she became quicker and motivated. She blossomed with happiness as the anxiety lifted and her shoulders relaxed. The more sorting we did, the more her unhappiness subsided and her cheeks flushed with colour and delight.

Once we finished sorting out her clothes, Camille broke down crying again. Initially, I thought she was upset at getting rid of some of her clothes, but then I realised it was because she was just so overjoyed with relief. Her face radiated happiness.

I was an emotional wreck, trying to keep my feelings contained and not sobbing relentlessly at the daughter's plight. I can picture her now, staring at me and then looking down in embarrassment. Softly she opened her heart and explained that she'd never had a sleep-over or friends staying for tea because she felt ashamed to let any of them see the mess of her home. Her feelings of shame and embarrassment stabbed my heart. For this girl to be 18 years old and never have a friend to stay was a wake-up call for me.

My children were having sleep-overs since they were toddlers. They enjoyed the experience of sharing their space with their friends, laughing and playing, creating fond memories. I couldn't comprehend all of the joy that she'd missed out on, with years of stress and anxiety, and all because her home was messy.

This experience was very upsetting but it made me appreciate how memories are so closely linked to our environment. If you love your space then you want to share it with others, but if you're embarrassed by it then you don't want anyone to see it and you're missing out on creating those precious memories and special times. I realised that a healthy and pleasant environment will keep you well both mentally and physically.

When I left the house with Amy, the car oozing bags of recycling, Camille was joyful and smiling. As I looked at her, I felt confident that she now had the skills to let go and organise her space. I felt rewarded knowing that she would no longer waste her time pushing stuff around her room and, most importantly, she no longer felt anxious about having friends over to stay. She'd learnt how to tidy up quickly so that her room would be perfectly presentable.

After 18 years, Camille had a space that she could only dream about before. She was a more confident and happier person now, which was evidenced by her cheerful smile as she stood in the doorway waving goodbye.

On the way home in Amy's car, I was feeling emotionally drained and physically exhausted, but also euphoric at the change in Camille. It helped me to realise how an organised home has so many physical and mental health benefits, and how a disorganised space can cause anguish, pain, loss of friendship and even isolation. I started to appreciate the link between interiors, emotions and wellness. I decided to focus on creating healthy organised homes because I wanted sons and daughters to feel empowered by their space and not overcome with the dismay of clutter.

MASTERING YOUR CLUTTER TRIGGERS

A practical and organised space can help you achieve physical, mental and emotional wellness. When your space is tidy, it stops you from tripping over things; it minimises distractions to keep you focused; it eases anxiety to help you feel calm; and it's healthier because it's easier to keep clean. It makes you feel better and your home looks attractive.

Tidying up, however, can often feel like a huge effort, time consuming, stressful and a burden. After the industrial revolution of the Victorian period, time and motion studies were popular because they looked at how we could work more productively. As technology advanced, our homes progressed as people wanted to get quicker and move faster. For example: a kitchen had gadgets and appliances, like a pop up toaster and washing machine, saving time and energy. The concept was that women would spend less time cooking and cleaning with more time to relax.

In today's modern home, even with the most recent technology, life is busy and time is still a luxury. As we're able to do things quicker and faster, we fill the gaps with other things; we socialise more, we exercise frequently, we work late or we run around with the kids. With the busyness of life, homes can quickly become messy and you don't want to spend time clearing up.

To create a perfectly presentable home and have the time to spend on the things you enjoy, the dream is for a spacious home that's organised. It will help to optimise your time by making it quick and easy to tidy up. But, just because a space is organised doesn't mean that it's going to get rid of the mess. I was with a couple who had a large fitted wardrobe in the master bedroom but, in the corner of the room was a hanging rail full of the husband's work shirts. The husband wanted his clothes to be separated, not because his wife had commandeered the wardrobe, but because it had become a jumbled mess. There were no drawers in the wardrobe so improvised shelves were hanging on the clothes rails and his shirts were getting creased.

Successful organisation needs to take into consideration the things that you have and why you like to keep them. When it's practical for you and your lifestyle, it will be perfectly presentable because, although your home gets untidy, there's a place for everything so it's quicker and more effective when tidying up. Effective organisation creates a space that's liveable, looks great and feels amazing.

When reviewing the organisation of your things, it's helpful to review why you keep specific types of objects. Once you understand why you keep things then you can put in place suitable storage that helps you tidy up effortlessly. It can also help you to realise why you find it difficult to let go of certain objects. When organising or decluttering your space, it's mindful to recognise that you don't have to throw away everything, just let go of the things that are causing you concern or making you feel anxious.

As William Morris, a British textile designer, said, "Have nothing in your house that you do not know to be useful, or believe to be beautiful."

JUST IN CASE:

The number one cause of clutter in the home is when you keep things because you want to feel ready and be prepared.

Rachel was a mother of three with a busy lifestyle, who wanted her home to be better organised. She'd suffered from a major illness, and as her time was spent recuperating, her home became cluttered.

They were both drowned in the sorrow. Now that she had recovered, she wanted to refresh her home and get rid of the mess. She was ready to make changes to create the spacious home that she longed for.

She had a stack of empty plastic margarine and ice cream tubs that she would fill with things until the lids bowed like hamster cheeks stuffed with sunflower seeds. As soon as one was full, she'd happily start filling the next one. They were filled with all of those little items that seem to clutter many homes, like paper clips and elastic bands, bits of toy parts, spare buttons and mini screwdrivers from a Christmas cracker. It's useful to have some of these items in the home but unless they're organised so that you can find them easily, it's just a box of junk. Rachel had a cupboard full of boxes of junk, neatly stacked but totally useless.

This survivor, war ration sentiment and Girl Guide *Be Prepared* mentality are common reasons for keeping items Just in Case. It's beneficial to be prepared and have spare items, like toilet rolls or light bulbs, but it becomes an issue when things overtake your space, cause concern or you lose track of what you have.

It was more time-consuming for Rachel to search for items than pop to the shops and buy them new. So, the boxes of junk just grew and grew. As the quantity of boxes expanded, Rachel had even more difficulty finding things, leaving her feeling lethargic and despondent.

For anyone who keeps items Just In Case, the key to a healthy organised home is to have a designated place for everything, so that you know where to put it back and can easily find it when that emergency calls. To organise the boxes for Rachel, I stored similar items together and added labels to identify their contents.

Part of the Just In Case personality is the inability to let things go because you feel as if you might run out of what you have. By having things ordered and in their allocated place, you can easily see when you're running short and need to stock up. It gives you the confidence that you are prepared for any eventuality. Being organised will also help to save money because you're not overspending on things that you already have.

SENTIMENTAL SAVER:

Sometimes we give a label of Just in Case when it's actually the Sentimental Saver personality. The Just in Case personality will keep things because they might be useful in the future, but the Sentimental Saver holds on to things because of an emotional attachment to the items.

For example, I had a student who came to my interior design course and, when we spoke about clutter, she shared with the group how she had a garage full of her daughter's soft toys just in case she wanted them back. The collection was so large that it was stopping her from putting her car in the garage and was a daily nuisance. When I challenged her and asked if she could clear her garage and give the toys back to her daughter, who had her own house, she was defensive, saying that the toys had to stay in her garage because the daughter had a small house.

Whatever solution I recommended, she had a comeback answer as to why the toys had to stay in her garage. Reading between her words and feeling her emotions, I could hear that she wanted to keep the toys because she had an emotional attachment to them. If she challenged her daughter to take the bundle of toys then her daughter might throw them away, which she would find emotionally upsetting and possibly even unbearable.

She wasn't ready to let go of the toys and their memories because she wanted to keep part of her daughter at home. She needed to recognise that the daily annoyance of having the toys in her garage was less of a nuisance than the anxiety and sense of loss she would feel if the toys were given away. Once she recognised this, it was no longer a nuisance to have the toys in her garage. She understood that it was her choice to store the toys and, when she was ready to let go of the attachment, she would be able to pass the toys to her daughter.

When organising your home, it's important to recognise the emotional connection that you have to things. It might be a prized certificate, a favourite item of clothing, a family photo, a piece of furniture, or a child's toy. It's worthwhile reviewing the items at least once a year to consider whether they are still vital to you and make your life happier. I have a teddy bear which was given to me by my grandmother when I was seven years old and has comforted both me and my children. His name is Tom and his soft brown fur has worn out in patches. It links me with my grandmother, my childhood and my children. He sits in the corner of my bedroom, reminding me of comfort and cuddles.

When you keep things because they have a sentimental value, then they either need to be visible so that you can see them every day, or stored in a place that's easy for you to access. When precious items are stored in the loft or at the back of a cupboard then they can become lost memories. Having the items close to hand enables you to experience the feelings of their warmth and joy.

CASH AWARE:

Cost and the value of items is another significant reason why you might decide to hold on to things.

I remember working with a retired gentleman who was reluctantly downsizing and needed help to clear out his workroom; a garage stuffed with carpentry tools and loving memories, like a wooden bench he crafted that was nestled amongst his garden shrubs, and a carved rocking horse heirloom that was being passed down generations to his grandchildren. Every time he picked up a tool, his eyes twinkled and a smile crossed his face. It was easy to see his devotion for the tools that had brought him so much pleasure and satisfaction.

Emotional drivers, such as fond memories, can be positive when they give us strength and determination to achieve amazing things. But they can also be negative when they hold us back from taking a leap into the new and unfamiliar, focusing on memories that hold us tight to the past.

The carpentry tools, and the precious memories they held, were connecting him to the past and happy times so he was finding it difficult, if almost impossible, to let go of them. The value of the items included their physical as well as their emotional value. This is the Cash Aware personality, where items have a financial as well as an emotional value, so it's difficult to let them go for a perceived low price.

Now, I'm not saying that you have to get rid of everything so that you live in a stark minimalist room but, like this gentleman, sometimes you're in a situation where you only have the space to keep the things that you feel are precious and meaningful. Unfortunately, he couldn't take the tools to his new house because space was critical and his hands were riddled with arthritis so he'd never be able to use them again.

I found a carpenter who wanted to buy the old tools and use them to lovingly create wooden furniture. It was the ideal scenario where my gentleman felt gratified that his carpentry tools would go on to create wonderful carvings for others to enjoy. It wasn't just important to sell the tools for their financial value, it was more important to find a home for their emotional value. This pleased the gentleman and he was able to move on knowing that the love and creativity he had put into the tools wouldn't be lost and forgotten.

STUCK IN A RUT:

As I was sharing this story with a student, she asked, "Why would someone pay you to throw out their things?" If you have healthy habits and feel comfortable de-cluttering then I can appreciate that it seems odd to call in someone to help you get rid of possessions. But, when you're stuck in a rut, the mess can feel overwhelming and you don't know where to start.

You can't see a way through the clutter and the chaos. You need guidance to break the back of the mess with advice on how to begin. You need professional guidance but, most importantly, you need emotional support.

Once you understand why you're connected to items, you can take a moment to appreciate what's important to your physical and emotional health, and what would be more beneficial for you to let go. It will help you out of the quagmire of indecision and chaos.

LETTING GO:

Every person is different and what you hold precious is therefore individual. Some things you might want to keep forever, but for others you know that you want to get rid of it but you're finding it difficult to part with. You may want to keep some things forever, but may find others difficult to part with even though they need to go. The answer to letting go is finding a way of moving on or breaking the emotional connection.

If you're a Just in Case personality, the key is to have clearly defined organisation so that you feel confident that you can find everything when needed. Storing items in labelled, clear-plastic boxes enables you to see things easily and find things quickly. You don't need to keep adding to the items once you can see that the box is full. You can let go because you've reduced any anxiety from feeling out of control. You feel organised and prepared.

If you're a Sentimental Saver, then it's important to recognise your emotional attachment to items. Reviewing your items yearly will help you recognise whether they still hold an important place in your life. To find out, you could put the things in the loft, a garage or a shed and see if you miss them. I used to do this with my children's old toys. They would go up into the loft for a few months and then I'd bring them back down. Usually the children would play with them for a few days, because of the novelty factor, but then they would be happy to give them to charity. Letting go is achieved when you appreciate that your emotions have moved on from that item and there's something better for you to love and care about.

If you're a Cash Aware personality, then it would be comforting to know that someone else can get just as much satisfaction and pleasure from the things you no longer need. You could give the items to your favourite charity, or sell them on an auction site and then use the money to buy something more suitable. For example, when a client downsized, her grandmother's vintage dresser no longer suited the modern home. She wanted to keep the memory of it without it taking up space in the small house. I recommended taking a photograph of the furniture and then buying something new that would be more appropriate for the new house. After she sold the dresser, she bought a vase that sits in the living room and reminds her of grandmother's favourite turquoise-coloured dress. Letting go was achieved because she passed on the emotional attachment through the physical sale of the item.

Mastering clutter and letting go isn't always quick and simple because it involves emotion, so you need to be in the right mindset to move on in your life. The first day of decluttering is always the most difficult because there's a pull to hold on to familiar things. After the first day, it should get quicker and feel enjoyable as you start to feel free from the mess and disorganisation.

Once you've mastered your clutter triggers, it will create a feeling of space and energy in your home, helping you to feel refreshed and invigorated. You'll be able to see the things you love and be able to find anything easily. As everything has a place in your home, it also becomes quick and easy to tidy up so that it's organised and you have more time to enjoy with loved ones.

YOUR MEMORIES TO CHERISH

This is your personal space to record the memories you never want to forget. You can take a moment to jot down, draw or scribble your thoughts and ideas.

CHAPTER 4

A CONFLICT OF IDEAS

How do you keep your identity and agree how a home should look when you share a space with others and there's a conflict of ideas?

When you move in with someone and you both want to assert your personality on the property, it's not a problem if you share the same personal style, but it can become a battleground if you have a difference of opinions and can't work out how to marry your ideas together. You both want to stamp your own identity on the place, but you just can't agree how you can unify your ideas to create a cohesive space.

Beth and Callum were in exactly that situation. Married for a couple of years, with two wrinkled Sharpei dogs, there was now an impasse because they couldn't decide how to bring their different styles together in the open-plan living and dining room.

I'd met Beth through a ladies' business group, where we connected immediately as she bounded towards me with her beaming smile. She had her own self-care, wellness company that helped women find balance in their lives. It was easy to see how her calming and thoughtful nature motivated the women, whilst her party spirit invigorated them.

Beth loved to travel with her husband and they'd been to many exotic locations. However, she would raise her eyebrows to me whenever she mentioned his collection of large and random mementos from their trips. In particular, there was an ornate screen from Indonesia and a carved elephant-shaped wooden table from India that she disliked because they didn't fit into her style of décor.

When Beth and Callum first moved into their 1970s house, they loved the clean lines and simplicity, but the living room was a square box and characterless. To furnish the living room they'd used the blood red leather sofa from Callum's bachelor flat and then added items to it from their travels. Beth was now starting to feel as if the holiday treasures were taking over the space and her home wasn't in balance. It had become a jumbled mixture of things that didn't go together and they were making the room feel cluttered and disorganised.

Beth disliked Callum's squeaky sofa because it dominated the lounge and felt cold in the winter. Callum liked his bachelor pad sofa because it was comfortable and full of memories, but he was happy to change it now that it didn't suit his more relaxed personal taste. The problem was that they couldn't agree on a new sofa as neither of them was willing to compromise. Beth and Callum had decorated the rest of their house successfully, but the challenge with their living room was a difference in styles. They didn't know how to create a space that they both loved. In a softly spoken voice of exasperation Beth told me, "We can't find a way to make the space work to reflect our different personalities."

Beth wanted to stamp her own style on the space rather than compromise with Callum's leftovers. She wanted a grey sofa in a soft fabric that was elegant and structured with sleek modern lines. Her dream was a calm and relaxing lounge with a soft cosy sofa where she could snuggle next to Callum.

The red leather sofa was a mark of Callum's youth, but the once-fashionable colour now felt harsh and aggressive. Callum's taste was casual and he preferred to change it for an oversized sofa with deep relaxing bed-like cushions. The modern 'show home' style that Beth loved seemed bland, stuffy and uninspiring to him. Callum wanted a relaxing room that was rustic, with ethnic touches and a place for his guitar.

Beth and Callum were fed up with the 'make do' space. Both of them wanted a calm, relaxing and homely space for entertaining friends and family. They were fed up living in a shabby room and desperate for a space that felt comfortable to them both and their individual taste. However, they couldn't see a way to compromise that would ensure each person kept their identity. Callum's taste was industrial and vintage whereas Beth's style was contemporary and elegant.

It was a tricky situation as the stalemate of ideas left the room with dated décor. They both wanted to redecorate but they weren't prepared to make any changes without being able to visualise how it would work and knowing where they would have to compromise. I've seen this situation many times and it usually occurs, as with Beth and Callum, when couples have polar opposite tastes in style.

As with any difference of opinions, it was important to focus on what they both liked and find the common ground to help solve the issue. It was a starting point on which to build a cohesive space that both partners would love and adore. Beth and Callum began by expressing their opinions so they could be heard and feel valued. Although they were hearing each other's thoughts, their opinions didn't feel valued because neither was willing to find a middle ground.

The starting point with Beth and Callum was to understand their keywords and how they wanted the space to feel. They agreed on *spacious, light and textured* with colours of teal blue to remind them of the ocean from their travels. Once they started focusing on what they both liked, they felt relieved and naturally began to compromise.

My first design for Beth and Callum's living space was working with the current furniture layout, but it didn't feel right because the flow of the space looked cramped and felt compromised. The dining space was squashed into a small confined area and the living space was spread around the open area of the room. Subsequently, the dining area felt restricted and the living area felt cold and unwelcoming.

Beth had told me specifically, multiple times, not to change the layout of the room, but I felt it would be a better use of the space if the room was flipped around. Dining in the open-plan area would provide Beth and Callum with more space for entertaining with their friends gathered around the dining table, and the living area in the cosy space would create a sense of calm and tranquillity for them to snuggle together on the sofa after a busy day.

Beth didn't want me to change the layout of the room because she was comfortable with how it looked already. She wasn't convinced that something different would feel better than the layout she already had. She was afraid to make a change that might upset her connection to the space. Often, familiarity stops us from making changes that might initially feel awkward, but they're frequently better than we'd imagined.

I was extremely nervous showing Beth the new design, but I knew that I had to be brave because it felt so right to me with the furniture swapped around. I could picture it in my mind. It's like augmented reality without me having to wear the funny goggles. If my ideas are fluid and cohesive then I will see the finished room like a picture, but if there is part of the design that doesn't work then it will be a bit fuzzy.

Beth and Callum's design was the perfect picture of excitement and tranquillity. My design brought together the personality of them both whilst keeping their identity and individuality in equal measures. The compromise was equal and fair because it was an eclectic mix of Beth's classic elegant style with Callum's quirky personal touches.

I was feeling confident about the changes I was recommending but I was worried how Beth would react. I was right to worry and feel anxious because she didn't like the design at all. She hated it. She told me over and over again how she didn't want me to change the furniture layout. Beth wouldn't even entertain the design to begin with. She wasn't angry with me but she was certainly disappointed, looking down and shaking her head. Callum had just wired the TV into the wall and now I was recommending a total rework of not just the furniture but also the electrics.

I wondered whether I should have played it safe and kept the furniture layout the same, but I knew in my heart that changing the furniture around would create a more social, calming and cosy space for Beth and Callum. It would give them everything they were searching for. I had to be true to my ideas and creativity. I had to go with my instinct and feelings, but now I was feeling miserable as I could see Beth's disappointment.

To help Beth come on board with my ideas, I had to help her understand the changes and how they would add value to her standard of living. Slowly, I went through the design in detail showing her images of how the space could look. I compared how the old layout was a compromise and the new layout would be an improvement.

The dining area was close to the kitchen but the space felt squashed and there wasn't enough room to entertain friends comfortably. In the new layout, it was only a couple of extra steps from the kitchen but the open plan area would provide valuable space to move around the dining table, even with all of their friends seated and enjoying a meal. The living area felt open and spacious but in being so cavernous it didn't feel cosy. Moving the living space to a more confined area of the room would provide an intimate space, and a door would solve the problem of Beth being able to see into the kitchen. The change of layout would create a cosy living area to help them relax.

For Beth to come to terms with my ideas, without committing to a permanent change, I encouraged her to try out the new layout. She just needed to swap the existing red sofa and dining table. After listening to my design details, she trusted me enough to try it out and was willing to swap them over. Bringing Beth on board with the new furniture layout was fundamental to success for the rest of the design. Although she was adamant that the new layout wouldn't feel comfortable for her, at least she was willing to try it out. I had a worrying wait.

When I spoke to Beth, a couple of weeks later, I was so relieved to hear that she absolutely loved the new layout. It wasn't at all what she expected. She was surprised how spacious it felt and how comfortable it was. A wave of emotions gushed over me as I felt elated and relieved. The worry drained from my senses as I poured myself a celebratory glass of wine.

With a more spacious dining area there was room for entertaining friends in comfort and the dogs could run around the table freely. It's always important to incorporate the needs of pets because they're valued members of the family. An open shelving unit, guarded by the carved elephant table, showcased the couple's treasures that they'd gathered from their travels. Callum loved it because he could see them all at a glance and Beth loved it because they were neatly organised. It incorporated both of their personalities so that neither felt as if they were compromising their individual style.

With a design that unified their styles, instead of having conflicting ideas for specific sofa styles, they were now able to consider all options. They both agreed to replace the blood red leather sofa with a luxurious teal blue velvet sofa. It softened the living area, creating a cosy and stylish place for Beth and Callum to relax. They felt comfortable in the new room. As Beth stretched out on the new sofa, she commented, "The space is lovely because it reflects both of our personalities and we don't have to compromise on style." Her kind words made me feel happy and rewarded after the initial anguish and worry of the design.

The first dinner party had been booked and they were looking forward to entertaining in their new stylish room. It was a place for them to enjoy creating memories to cherish with friends and family.

CREATING UNITY

Sharing a space with someone else, even when you love them so deeply, can be challenging. You have different backgrounds, tastes and style so creating a space of unity is not always easily achievable. I think sometimes, because we love the person, we expect there to be natural compromises but it's common to find sticking points in the home where disagreements occur. It could be a difference on opinions concerning the colour, wallpaper, sofa style or even the use of space.

I was once asked to review the living room for a couple where the husband had moved into the wife's house. He wanted space for his books and to stamp his own identity on the living room.

It was her home that she'd grown accustomed to. She didn't know how to make space for her new husband because she was comfortable with everything just as it was. She was a teacher and in the living room was a large shelving unit that stretched along the full length of one wall, which cascaded with gifts from her students. She had lovingly kept all of them because she was worried that giving them away would mean that she didn't care about them. The gifts themselves had little monetary value but the thoughts behind them were recognition of her effort and symbols of her success. Emotionally they were valued, but physically they were cluttering the shelves and taking up space.

Talking her through the gifts one by one enabled her to appreciate that she didn't even like the '*You Are The Best Teacher*' plaque or the '*Number 1 Teacher*' trophy, so giving the gifts to charity would feel refreshing and also free up valuable storage space for her husband's books. Keeping a photo of the sentimental gifts would be more pleasurable and less stressful than having the items cluttering up her home.

Her husband affectionately said, "I don't want a lot of space, just *some* space." Now that they were married and he was living in her house permanently, he wanted to feel as if he at least had some identity in the home. He wanted to feel as if he belonged.

When people join together to live in one home, they need to find a way of harmonising the space with their personal possessions. To the person who owns an item, it is valuable treasure that they don't want to live without. But to the other person, it can often be viewed as junk and clutter. To create unity, the compromise is to allocate a dedicated space to each person. It doesn't matter how large or small the space is because it just needs to be your personal space. It might be that you each have your own room, a drawer in a cupboard or a shelf on the wall. For the teacher and her husband, the solution was to restyle the living room shelves so that there was space for him and space for her. He would have room for his books and she would be able to display her collections.

The teacher's predicament was simple to address because the belongings were restricted to a shelving unit, but what happens when one person's possessions start to dominate the house? It can lead to arguments, resentment and even a breakdown of the relationship if left unresolved.

I was asked by one of my students to help her out of a tricky situation as her husband was a Lego collector. Now, that in itself isn't a problem but it was starting to take over the family home. Ava no longer had a guest bedroom because it was rammed with Lego. Now that the guest bedroom was stuffed to bursting, the living room was also starting to become a storage room for the plastic building bricks. She felt as if she had nowhere to relax and could no longer invite family over to stay. As her home became more and more cluttered, she was embarrassed to invite friends over for coffee with playdates for the kids. Her husband's obsession was causing constant arguments and Ava couldn't see any way of remedying the problem.

Once the arguments start, it can be an overwhelming and scary situation. You care for the person that you're living with and don't want to offend them, but you also don't want their possessions dominating the space. You want peace and harmony in your home, not a battleground, but there's often an impasse of ideas and little compromise. It's stalemate.

Looking around Ava's home, I could see that there wasn't enough space within the property to store the vast Lego collection. Her husband was adamant that he wouldn't reduce his beloved collection and they couldn't afford to move to a bigger house. Additional storage is one of the main reasons given when moving to a larger house. Upgrading their home for a larger property would have helped Ava in the short term but once the collection took hold, it would begin to swamp any new house. She would have the same problem with lack of space but her husband would have a larger collection.

Her only realistic options would be to either reduce the size of their garden with a purpose-built shed or pay for off-site storage. After careful consideration and much discussion, both Ava and her husband decided off-site storage would be the best solution. It would be an additional expense, but it was worth it to stop the arguments and create unity in the home. Although they now had off-site storage, Ava would still have to set boundaries as to how much Lego she would allow into the family home if she wanted to keep her bedrooms and living space clutter free.

Finding the common ground is key to unlocking a stalemate. Ava was willing to have some Lego in her home but she didn't want it to be used as a storeroom. Her husband wanted to have some Lego at home and a personal area to keep his collection. They both agreed on the amount of Lego to be kept in the house, and it was stored in a dedicated cupboard.

Discord frequently relates to the amount of space each person has for their things, but it can also apply to personal style and décor. It often occurs when one person wants a traditional style and the other is more modern, or when one person likes bold colours but the other prefers soft tones, or even when one person likes pattern but the other prefers plain and simple.

To find harmony and create unity, a good starting point is to find your similar values. You might both value eco-friendly and focus on natural, organic textures. You might both value simple styles and focus on sleek elegant furniture. Or, you might both prefer geometry and choose precise linear patterned wallpaper.

An alternative compromise is to choose a colour that you both love. For example, a colour from your travels that relates to happy memories will help create a successful interior where you both feel comfortable. If you can't agree on one single colour choice then you could choose a neutral colour base (black, grey, white, beige, cream, brown) for the larger items such as curtains and sofas, and incorporate a pop of colour in your accessories. Choosing accessories together, such as a beautiful painting, will help to signify your solidarity and companionship. Having something shared will help you both feel valued with a special bond to each other. It will help to create a unified space that you both enjoy.

There will always be something that you both like and can use as the basis for your room inspiration. When you're both connected to the space, you feel as if you belong, which brings feelings of harmony and contentment to your home. It becomes a space that you both enjoy and want to share with those you love.

<u>YOUR MEMORIES TO CHERISH</u>

This is your personal space to record the memories you never want to forget. You can take a moment to jot down, draw or scribble your thoughts and ideas.

CHAPTER 5

A SENSE OF BELONGING

Moving into a new house is initially exciting because you've finally got your own space with hope and expectations that it will be everything you've always dreamt of. For most people, moving house brings the luxury of added space.

As well as all of this beautiful new space, you've also inherited the décor from the previous owners, which either will be a blessing or an eyesore. If you've inherited a style that you love then that's unusual because there's often something that you want to change to make the new home individual and unique to you. It might be a new-build house that's full of magnolia paint and you want to add a splash of vibrant colour. It could be a period house that's been stripped of its features and you want to give it back some character. It may even be a townhouse with dated décor and you want to freshen it up with modern touches. You have the space and now you want it to be your home that reflects your personality.

When Clare called me, she was so excited to share the news that she'd moved into a new home. It was a quaint English cottage with a thatched roof, trailing roses around the door and a rambling garden. Although the house looked lovely on the outside, Clare was embarrassed by the interior she'd inherited. The dated decor was making her feel anxious and embarrassed to invite friends over to show them her new home.

Clare didn't know where to begin to fix the problems that were making her feel unsettled. She absolutely loved all of the new space and room to move about, but she struggled to visualise when it came to decorating. She couldn't see how it would look when finished; she didn't feel confident choosing colours and she couldn't afford to make expensive mistakes.

As I walked up the cobbled path to Clare's new house, it was like being in an idyllic dream that's picture perfect. The house greeted me as I picked my way through the cottage garden full of English plants – hollyhocks, daisies and poppies – the delicate flowers straining for the sunshine and bobbing in the wind. The old-style plants reminded me of home, where my father loved to grow similar flowers that would tumble over the brick walls of the back yard in the summertime. It felt exciting and comforting walking towards the stone-built cottage.

Clare greeted me in a small but practical hallway that led straight into a spacious kitchen that was flooded with light from a modern, glass conservatory at one end. Oak shaker-style units wrapped around the kitchen, encasing a traditional Aga cooker. It was exactly what you might expect from a cottage kitchen and was the family-entertaining space that Clare had always dreamt of. The combination of light and space made it a place the whole family would enjoy. It was the reason she bought the cottage.

As I stepped into the living room, it was a different story. The room was barren and lifeless, making it feel like a scene from an old western movie, where tumbleweed rolls down the deserted street. It felt unloved and uninviting. It made me shiver with cold.

Clare wanted it to be bright and cheerful, but the dark and gloomy space was making her feel worried and stressed. She had nowhere to relax and unwind. As a busy working mum, she needed a homely living room as quickly as possible. Clare wanted to feel settled, but she didn't know where to start.

This was an important room where Clare would be entertaining, so I wanted it to be exciting and invigorating, a special place for creating memories with friends and family.

Fortunately, there were some great features in the room, like the wood-burning stove nestled into a brick inglenook fireplace, but overall the room felt dark and sad. Sometimes this happens when the colour scheme is unbalanced, the furniture is badly positioned or the lighting is inadequate. With diamond-leaded windows on three of the walls, and the sun streaming through the patio doors, there was no obvious reason why the room should feel so dark and cold.

Looking around Clare's living room, I could see that the curtains she'd inherited were swamping the windows, obstructing the sunlight from flooding into the living room. The duck egg blue curtains looked as if they were once a beautiful rich colour, but they'd now lost their shine. The colour was both muted and dull, sapping light from the room, making the space feel drab and dark. The curtains were old, wrinkled and dreary, so it was time for a change.

Looking at the barren living room, it was difficult to see Clare's style because it was devoid of her character. Clare looked at me with hope, keen for me to create a living room that felt special, a space that had personality and a place where she could relax. Having only just met Clare, and with no inspiration from her room, it was a daunting experience conjuring up ideas for her dream home.

Looking at Clare's personal style for inspiration, I could see that her dress was plain and simple. It had subtle detail with soft gentle colours. Her outfit didn't shout 'look at me' but it also didn't pale into insignificance. She looked elegant, neat and friendly, so I decided that these were to be my keywords for the design. I wanted to create an elegant room for Clare to entertain her loved ones, choosing simple stylish pieces and adding a touch of colour to energise the room.

My inspiration came in the form of fabric. Being brought up on material, from my father working in a cotton mill and my grandmother teaching me how to sew, I suppose it's my go-to place for ideas. I love the textures, the balance of colours and the feeling of cloth. Whether it's a new pair of curtains, a cosy throw or a fluffy cushion, changing the fabric will refresh a room instantly. It's a quick win, so it's a great starting point when you move into a new house and want to feel settled.

For Clare's living room, I chose a beautiful curtain fabric with colourful red poppies. In keeping with the country-cottage style, the flowers were bright and cheerful on a clotted cream background. The traditional country pattern brought a sense of gracefulness to the space whilst the poppies connected the living room to the surrounding floral garden. Being able to touch the fabric and see the pattern made it easy for Clare to understand the colour scheme and visualise her dream lounge. She loved it.

Whilst discussing colour for the living room walls with Clare, she mentioned her son's bedrooms because she was worried that the boys were also finding it difficult to relax into their new home. Settling into their new home was proving difficult for all of the family. Although the cottage was attractive on the outside, the previous owners had left their personal taste and style behind them. It was a colour scheme and décor that didn't suit Clare or her family.

When you move into a new house with decoration that isn't to your taste it can be exciting because there's the opportunity to stamp your own style on the property. It can feel exhilarating and fun. For Clare, however, she wasn't confident with decorating and had little time to dedicate to the house, so she felt overwhelmed at the prospect of it. She was apprehensive about choosing colours, which is why she often opted for neutrals and pastel shades.

For her children, in particular, she didn't want to get it wrong. The boys were struggling to sleep and didn't want to have any friends over to play because the bedrooms were a riot of pink. From her furrowed brow, I could see that Clare was concerned. She said that the boys were usually sociable children with many friends who always had play dates in their old house. Although the boys now had the luxury of a bedroom each, instead of sharing, they were embarrassed by what they called the 'girly' decor. The boys were worried that their friends would tease and make fun of them, so they preferred not to invite them home to play.

When Clare showed me the sons' bedrooms I did take a step backwards with disbelief because it was full-on pink. I absolutely adore pink, but this was to the extreme with sugary pink paint on the walls, frilly pink curtains and even pink floral lampshades. It should have been an exciting time for the boys now that they had their own room, but they were sad because the space didn't reflect their personalities. It's no wonder they were feeling unsettled and unhappy with their new rooms. They wanted the comfort and familiarity of their old bedroom.

Standing beside Clare in one of the bedrooms, she turned to me with a troubled face and said, "Let's do a quick makeover of the boys' bedrooms before we tackle the living room, because I don't want them feeling so sad." Clare wanted to put her own dream on hold to nurture her children. A mother's love is always beautiful to behold.

The boys were hyper-excited when Clare told them they were going to have their rooms designed to be exactly how they wanted.

They jumped with happiness. As we sat down at the dining table together, their arms were laden with their favourite books and toys. Chatting excitedly, their minds opened up to a world of possibilities as they shared their ideas with me. I absolutely love designing for children because they're a mine of creative ideas. You just have to sieve them a little to make sure you find the nuggets of gold.

I was eager to show the boys their bedroom designs full of colour and excitement. Using high-street products, personal colours and heaps of imagination, my designs were going to create an instant makeover. I wanted the rooms to be full of fun, lively and invigorating. The boys loved my initial ideas so much that they took a picture of my design to school and proudly showed their friends, taking bookings for the big reveal. I felt elated being given that opportunity to help turnaround their outlook, helping to make their move a positive and exhilarating experience.

The youngest boy had dreamt of a bedroom full of sea monsters. He loved all kinds of animals in the water so his bedroom was painted a cooling beautiful blue. To compliment the sea monster theme, I sourced an urchin style lampshade and added a shoal of exotic fish stickers that swam around the sea blue walls. When it was finished, he ran into the bedroom screaming with delight.

The oldest boy's bedroom was my favourite design because he wanted dinosaurs to roam his room. He loved collecting fossils and knew the name of every dinosaur, with his favourite being the formidable Tyrannosaurus Rex. How was I going to get a dinosaur to roam his bedroom, particularly when it was a small loft bedroom with awkward angles and compromised on space?

To make the room feel spacious, I created a palate of pale grey on all of the walls and ceiling. This is a great trick to iron out any awkward edges because you can't see where one wall starts and the next begins. It was a lovely canvas as a backdrop for dinosaurs. To make it feel as if a dinosaur was walking in the room, I sourced a large T-Rex wall sticker that spanned across two walls, towering up from the floor and looming onto the ceiling, roaring with menace. From the son's top bunkbed, he would be able to look the dinosaur straight in the eye.

When the room was finished, as his eyes scanned the T-Rex, his head gently tipped upwards and, with his eyes wide with happiness, he turned to me and politely said, "Thank you." Looking into his angelic face, I felt overwhelmed with his delight.

With both boys now having a room to show off, it wasn't long before they were inviting their friends over, smiling and laughing with joy. Clare was delighted with their happiness as they were sleeping so much better and feeling settled in their new home.

It was now time to finish the makeover of the living room so that Clare could also relax and unwind in her new home. As the curtains were being made in the beautiful poppy fabric, we shopped for furniture. It was fun shopping with Clare, helping her choose a grey sofa and building her confidence with interiors.

As we picked out the perfect grey velvet fabric for her new sofa, it reminded me of time with my grandmother. I was passing on knowledge that I'd learnt as a four year old: how the different fabric weights would change the sofa experience – a light-weight velvet for a soft and cosy feeling, and a heavier, stiffer velvet for a more formal and precise look. It was all coming back to me.

I received a lovely card from Clare saying how tasteful, elegant and cosy the living room was. She felt settled and comfortable, having her friends and family over to celebrate in style.

A NEW HOME

You've finally found a place to call home but now you're not sure where to start decorating or how to fit your old stuff into your new place. This was the problem for Daisy who called me over to review her new home because she'd moved from South Africa to England and was struggling to squeeze her large sofas into the quaint cottage. Moving into a new home is often unsettling, but moving to a different country adds a deeper level of emotion and anxiety. It can be upsetting and stressful, so it's important to create a home that feels welcoming and relaxing as quickly as possible.

In South Africa, Daisy's home was spacious and open. By contrast, in England, her cottage felt small and cramped. She said that it was like squeezing a giant into a hobbit house. Daisy wanted her cottage to feel comfortable, a place to help her feel at home.

As I entered the living space, the room felt awkward with the furniture dumped as if it had fallen from a removal van. I've seen many rooms looking lost and feeling unloved because it's challenging to fit old stuff into a different space. Like Daisy's living space, it usually happens when you've just moved into a new house and you don't know where to place things. The space becomes transient rather than an enjoyable, cosy place.

Daisy couldn't afford to replace the sofas, because the majority of family finances had gone into the move and buying the quaint English village cottage. She had to use the furniture that they brought with them and it needed to work in the living space. As well as the practicality of keeping the existing furniture, Daisy didn't want to get rid of her sofas because they reminded her of South Africa and the lifestyle she loved. She was emotionally attached to them.

The solution for Daisy was to utilise the whole of the living space instead of pushing the sofas into a corner of the room. To try and make a room feel more spacious, furniture is often pushed against a wall or squeezed into the corner of a room. The perception is that, the more floor space you can see, the more spacious a room will feel because there's a gap of nothingness in the middle.

To create a sense of space, however, the solution is not necessarily to leave big open gaps in your room. Having an expanse of nothingness in the middle of the room creates a void of emotion like an empty lifeless corridor. As all of the interest is focused around the perimeter of the room, the middle of the room looks barren and can become disconnected with the rest of the space.

The solution is to position furniture so that it allows you to easily move around the room whilst creating a warm and welcoming scene. Each room becomes a story, using furniture as the characters, décor as the backdrop and accessories to enhance the plot.

For Daisy, I placed the sofas into the middle of the living space and a wood-burning stove was installed against the central wall to create a feature fireplace. The room now had a focal point, creating a cosy place to relax and unwind. With the sofas moved away from the walls, the natural stonework of the cottage could be appreciated, adding texture to the scene. To complete the story, Daisy's South African drums were positioned as side tables and her ethnic rug adorned the floor at the foot of the sofas. With her African art proudly hanging on the walls, it was now the perfect place to remind her of home. It was her sanctuary. Repositioning the furniture and creating a story using accessories from her homeland helped Daisy to feel settled into her new home whilst creating a nurturing place to enjoy with her family.

As Daisy experienced, squeezing furniture into a different style of house can be particularly difficult, especially when it involves a different country. How do you choose furniture that suits the new home and fits in perfectly when properties are different?

I was involved with a lovely group of international expat ladies, whose husbands were temporarily working in England. Each family had been uprooted from their home country and it was interesting to see the dynamics of their lifestyle as they coped with a new country and a temporary new house. The majority of ladies were in the country for a couple of years, in which time they settled in and sorted out schools for their children whilst building new friendships. Then, just as quickly, they prepared to move out. They had the move in/move out routine down to a fine art.

The majority of their homes were rented by the husbands' firm, so the ladies were constrained by the décor and structure of the space. All of the rented houses were painted a cream colour, from the walls to the neutral carpet and impersonal bathroom tiles; it was all pale and neutral. The houses were rented unfurnished and often devoid of personality, a blank canvas. The only way they could add a sense of homeliness to the space was through furniture and accessories, incorporating a few personal items from home.

One lady in particular took a camel wherever she went. Not a real one, I hasten to add, but still quite large. It was about 3 feet tall, just less than a metre, made out of wicker and adorned with colourful fabric. Its bandy legs made it difficult for it to stand straight but it looked beautiful to her. The camel's hump was adorned with a vibrant pattern and exotic coloured material. Each time she moved house, it was carefully packaged and then given pride of place in her new home. She knew that it didn't fit in with the style of her modern English room but she loved it all the same. Her husband disliked it and hoped that it would be lost on each subsequent move, but it was her comfort blanket and a cheerful friend she could rely on to help her feel settled. It helped her to feel grounded in a strange place.

Most of the ladies brought a few treasured items from home, but the majority of furniture was purchased in England. As the ladies were only in the country for a couple of years and the space not being their own, they didn't want to invest in the décor or buy expensive new furniture. Ingeniously, they created a group where ladies moving out of the country could list furniture and accessories that they didn't want to take back home, and ladies moving into the country could pick up items that would fit into the style and shape of English homes. It was an international swap shop.

The swap shop was a quick and effective way of moving into the country because they didn't have to spend hours searching for suitable items. It also helped them settle into the country quicker because they could focus on the family instead of worrying about the home. The ladies would entertain each other with afternoon tea in their new home, proud to show off their English style with fine finger sandwiches and cream scones served on Wedgewood plates. They felt settled and relaxed.

Choosing the right furniture for your home can sometimes feel daunting because the choice is vast and you don't want to make an expensive mistake. To help you make the right choice, focus on the keywords of how you want the space to feel. For example, the sofa that you choose for a modern style would be different to a traditional style. The modern sofa would have sleek lines with an angular frame, whereas the traditional sofa would have curves and finishing touches like frills or button back. You can also think about how you want your room to feel. For example, if you want it to feel warm and welcoming then you could choose a fabric sofa with soft luxurious velvet, whereas if you want it to be practical and family friendly then a leather sofa could be a better choice.

Once you've decided on the style and placement of furniture, the main characters of your scene, you can then work your way through choosing the décor and complimentary accessories. In this way, your budget is firstly apportioned for the expensive items with the remainder then allocated to the more affordable objects. Deciding on the large items first also ensures a more cohesive design because the type of wallpaper and accessories you choose will complement the furniture colour and style.

If you're searching for ideas and inspiration, to help you decorate your new home, you could take inspiration from your friends or neighbours. This is particularly useful if they have a similar taste or the same style of property as your own. Alternatively, there are many interior design shows with all of the latest trends and designer fashions. If you haven't got time to visit a show then you might prefer to read an interior magazine. Choose a magazine that suits the style you want to create in your home – traditional or modern, country cottage or loft apartment, homely or spacious – and review what it is about the interior that you like. You can then create a design for your home using the ideas you've gathered.

Just be mindful if you directly copy an image from a magazine because it won't always suit you or your home. I had one lady who asked me to review her home because she'd redecorated her open plan kitchen/dining/living space to look exactly like her inspirational magazine photo. The kitchen was the same, the dining table was an exact copy and even the accessories on the dresser were identical to the image. It was lovely, but she didn't like it and it wasn't her dream room. There was something missing. The problem was that it lacked her personality.

Although you're taking inspiration from others, creating a new home that feels welcoming, comfortable and stylish should still have your personality and individual flair incorporated into the design. It will include personal items from your history, travels or new experiences. It will then be your story and your unique home to love and cherish.

YOUR MEMORIES TO CHERISH

This is your personal space to record the memories you never want to forget. You can take a moment to jot down, draw or scribble your thoughts and ideas.

CHAPTER 6

TIME TO CALL IT A DAY

Sometimes you might have to move out of your home when you're not quite ready to leave. It might be a time when you're going through a break-up, downsizing because your home is too large after the children have left, or suffering an illness and need to move to a property that's more accommodating.

When you don't want to move out but you have to move on, it can be an emotional time full of sadness, anger or despair as you're forced to leave your home. At a time of uncertainty, as your world turns upside down, you can experience a loss of security as the comfort of your home is taken away. Even if a home has become a place of arguments, you're still sad to let it go because it used to be a place of love and happiness.

Judith and her husband had agreed to separate because, although they still cared for each other, they no longer loved each other. They wanted to move on with their own lives, so it was time to sell the family home.

When you've invested love and affection into your home, your family and your relationship, it's a heart-wrenching decision to make. Judith and her husband were upset to have to say goodbye to the house they'd lovingly created together, but they knew it was the right decision for them and their teenage children. But how can you make the move as stress-free as possible, not just for you but also for your family and loved ones?

Judith's home was a large converted barn hugging a rambling Grade II listed property, with part of it believed to date back to medieval times of 1665, that they'd lovingly restored and redecorated.

It was full of character and charm. Although it was very attractive on the outside, unfortunately it was disappointing on the inside.

It was a warren of rooms and, as Judith said when she introduced herself to me, "My estate agent said it needs decluttering and a spruce up. In particular, I have to make the upstairs look more appealing, to redress the imbalance between the huge and interesting downstairs and the smaller upstairs."

Judith was initially shocked by her estate agent's comments, but she was also practical and knew that she had to do something about the presentation of her home if she wanted to sell it and move on with her life. She didn't want to live in limbo with her husband. She wanted her freedom.

When I first met Judith she was feeling worried and anxious, overwhelmed by the changes that needed to be made but hopeful they would attract a buyer who would love her home just as much as she once did. The property had already been on the market for some time, with very few viewings and no offer in sight. Judith wanted to sell the house as quickly as possible, but it was proving a struggle with the décor holding her back.

As I stepped into the conservatory entrance, I could see sadness in the home. A wing-backed chair was pushed into a corner like a lonely person sitting and waiting for company. Its once-vibrant fabric was dull and lacklustre, tattered from cat's scratches and festooned in fluffy, white dog hairs. It looked unloved, abandoned and unappealing as a first impression for potential buyers.

When you've lived in your home for a while, it becomes difficult to see the space in the way that buyers might view it. You love your home so why shouldn't someone else love it just as much as you do?

Why can't they see past your furniture and accessories to appreciate the adorable property beneath? It's because most buyers only see the property as it's presented to them. They don't have your lifetime of memories attached to it. They see a tatty ragged chair in an otherwise empty conservatory, but you see a chair where you used to sit and read to your daughter as your son rode his bike up and down the flagstones. You have so many fond memories. To you it's perfect, but to a buyer it could be disappointing.

As we moved into the dark, country-style kitchen with its traditional blue Aga, I was greeted by a tall, slender girl with golden hair. "What are you doing here? Go away!" she said scornfully, as I entered the room. I was shocked and stood in silence for a moment. Never before had I been greeted like this.

"Sally!" retorted Judith, as she shifted uncomfortably from one foot to the other, embarrassed by her daughter's reaction. Sally swiftly picked up her plate of food and stormed out of the kitchen, glaring at me and slamming the door behind her.

Sally was Judith's 17-year-old daughter. Judith explained that Sally didn't want her parents to split up and was delighted that the family home was struggling to sell. Sally was hoping that her parents would rekindle their love for each other, but Judith knew there was no going back. Her daughter had to face reality, but she was making Judith's life difficult and was soon to vent her wrath on me.

As Judith shared more of the family home with me, it became obvious why it was struggling to sell. It looked unloved and abandoned as the house was showing symptoms of their dwindling relationship. Bulging bookcases lined the hall, stuffed with memories that mattered to neither of them now. A family photo was hanging from a tarnished frame, the once smiling faces now faded from the sun and covered in dust.

Reaching the master bedroom, I was preparing myself for the worst. In situations of separation, the master bedroom is usually dated and lifeless because it's not been decorated or cared for in quite a while. Judith's master bedroom was angry and aggressive, with blood red shouting from every pore of the room. The curtains were red, the walls were red and the bedding was red. It was bleeding red like a murder scene. The bedroom had gone past the point of love and romance and would scare off any potential buyer.

For me, the saddest part of the master bedroom was a single bedside table sitting forlorn. No longer could it be joined with its mate, one either side of the bed, as they were separated to different rooms – one for him and one for her. Judith and her husband were sleeping in separate rooms, with separate beds, contemplating their separate lives. Although this was the best practical solution for Judith and her husband, it did make the master bedroom feel unloved. Particularly in a master bedroom, furniture is paired to show bonding and unity, but a single bedside table will reflect loneliness to any potential buyer.

Judith didn't know where to begin with sorting out the house. It was overwhelming when mixed with the anxiety from the breakdown of her marriage and the stress of her daughter's wrath.

When you're overwhelmed with life, it can often be difficult to think straight so, to make the process as easy as possible for Judith, I presented her with a task list detailing exactly what she needed to do in every room. It gave Judith a step-by-step guide. It helped her to focus and motivated her to pack up things and have a major clear out. Every time she had a major throwing out, it alleviated her anxiety and helped her feel empowered with courage and strength to take the next step.

As Judith was busy sorting and clearing out the possessions that she'd gathered over her lifetime, slowly separating her life from her past with her husband, I focused on decorating and restyling her home, making each room appealing for buyers.

In the master bedroom, I altered the proportions of the angry red, replacing it with a neutral clotted cream colour as the focus, with red as the accent colour. Crisp cream sheets and a textured throw substituted the red bedding. The angry red wall was relaxed with a large cream floral picture and the room was softened with a large, cream fluffy rug. The changes helped to soften the overall room, making it feel romantic and bringing back the love.

As Judith became happier, brighter and more positive about a successful sale of the family home, Sally became ever more gloomy and obstructive. She demanded more time and attention from her mother, slowing down her decluttering and delaying her packing. Every time I visited, Judith would apologise for her daughter's behaviour as her verbal abuse towards me increased.

The day I was due to style Sally's bedroom was her most prolific outburst. With Judith wanting to appease her, and Sally being stubborn, I was compromised on the changes I could make to her bedroom. In other areas of the home, I had a free rein – creating a welcoming seating area in the conservatory entrance and toning down the ox-blood red in the master bedroom. But Sally was limiting any changes I could make to her bedroom.

I could have disregarded Sally and totally redesigned her bedroom, however, she was already showing emotional distress at the thought of her parents splitting. A drastic change could make her feel even more unsettled and angry, so I thought it wise to make the minimum amount of changes that would create the greatest impact.

As I started to make my way upstairs, Judith looked up from a packing box and said, "Be warned." I wondered what Sally had in store for me and when I reached her bedroom I exploded with laughter. I think Sally was hoping that I would be angry and annoyed, but the sign she'd put on her bedroom door was more hysterical than frightening.

In the middle of Sally's door was a picture of Moaning Myrtle, from *Harry Potter*, which was supposed to be a likeness of me. Emblazoned across the face of Moaning Myrtle was a thick red cross with the words GET OUT AND STAY OUT!

As I stepped into Sally's bedroom, I was intrigued to look at myself in her mirror, curious to see if there was a likeness. With my round glasses, black tunic top and dark brown hair in bunches, it was comical to see Moaning Myrtle reflecting back at me. At that moment, Judith appeared to console me.

I wasn't upset by the graffiti poster, or being likened to Moaning Myrtle, but I was feeling sad because this was the face of Sally's anger. I was the facilitator of her parent's separation and she was desperate for me to leave. At least she was expressing her emotions and vocalising her concerns, but it was saddening to see her desperation.

I had to empathise with Sally and her emotional stress because she knew her family home would soon sell. Already she could see her mother becoming happier, more confident and independent. Soon her life would be in turmoil as her family home, her security blanket, would be whipped away from her.

On our last day together, Judith had a spring in her step and a smile on her face as she said, "The house looks fantastic and I love it.

My husband is extremely happy too. We are still going to sell, but it is a far more pleasant environment."

With a heavy heart, Sally had reconciled herself to her parent's separation. She knew that she couldn't stop it happening, so she decided on a university course that would help her create her own fresh start and new beginnings.

The makeover had not only brought happiness to the family home, but it also brought a sense of calm to Judith and Sally. The property sold and they were looking forward to their next life adventure.

MOVING HOUSE

There are many reasons why a property struggles to sell but, it's often manifested with a lack of buyers, a low offer price or even no offer in sight. It can be frustrating and upsetting because you feel as if your life is on hold while you wait for your property to sell.

As you anxiously sit and wait for the doorbell to ring, you wonder why buyers aren't knocking down your door to see your lovely home. And, why are the buyers who visit your property offering you a low price? Don't they see the value of your home and all of the renovations you've made? You've invested time, energy and your savings to create the home of your dreams.

Often a property struggles to sell because it doesn't correlate to your buyers' expectations. It represents your dreams and not their dreams. I remember being called to review a home that was going up for sale. It was a traditional Victorian period home and as I stepped through the front door, it was oozing character. A long narrow corridor greeted me with dusty parquet flooring and intricately patterned wallpaper clung to every wall. It was an explosion of the senses.

As I stepped into the dining room, coldness swamped me. Not because it was physically cold but because it looked unloved and forgotten. The room was wrapped with dark red vintage wallpaper, making the room feel dark and oppressive. In the middle of the room was a cheap-looking, circular, pine dining table accompanied by a white plastic chair. The single chair looked lonely and abandoned. When styling such a large family home for sale, one lonely chair symbolises, as we say in Lancashire, Billy No Mates. Looking sad and forlorn, it would turn away any potential buyer. Ideally, there would have been several chairs placed around the table, giving the impression of a gathering of hearts and a welcoming space for entertaining friends and family.

The high street table was a cause for concern because it didn't reflect the price point of the property. Buyers wanted to see their dream home and flat-packed furniture wasn't up to the mark. They had expectations to see classy furniture in the expensive property. The pine table wouldn't entice buyers and they'd instantly disconnect.

Styling a property for sale focuses on creating the right perceptions and a welcoming ambience. You want potential buyers to fall in love with your home as soon as they see it. With many buyers viewing property online, it's critical to make a great first impression to entice them to your door. Once they're inside the property, they then need to feel emotionally connected to your home.

When I was asked to review a three-bed house, that was attracting young professional couples eager to make it their first home together but owned by a mature couple wanting to downsize, the property wasn't selling. The house was spotlessly clean and in good order, but the décor was chintzy floral fabrics, bright colourful carpets and a collection of small fussy ornaments. The young professional buyers had grown up in a different design period with modern décor, simple colours and large statement accessories. Although the property looked great on the particulars, the buyers found it difficult to see the house beneath the décor. Although perfect for the mature couple, it didn't suit their style and expectations. All they could see was clutter and flounce which was not at all to their taste and liking. They walked in the front door full of hope, but they walked out feeling disappointed.

When selling a property it's extremely important to understand your buyer and what they might expect to see from your home. To achieve a sale, the period property had to be simplified with plain curtains and modern paint colour so that it was in keeping with the expectations of the young professional couples.

Another question to ask yourself is: what do buyers expect to see as they walk around your home? If you're selling a three-bedroom property, then a buyer expects to see three clearly defined bedrooms. I know this sounds obvious, but it's often overlooked with one of the bedrooms as an office and another as a junk room. Both of these scenarios will devalue your property because the buyer can't physically see three good-sized bedrooms. The buyer will only see what's presented in front of them. They often can't visualise the potential of a room and how it could be used.

I was asked to review a large five-bed family home that was struggling to sell. It had been on the housing market a while, wasn't attracting buyers, and those that did come to look around were suggesting comically low offer prices. However, it wasn't a joke to the family trying to sell and move out. The husband's job was relocating and the children were moving school so the property had to sell, and it had to sell quickly so that the family could move on with their life.

The property was a lovely large house in a beautiful rural location, so why wasn't it selling? As I entered the family home I could see that it needed a little tidy up to make the house look appealing to buyers. When someone is looking to buy your home, they don't want to be presented with your daily drudgery of the kid's toys lying around and the washing stacking up. They don't want to be reminded of daily life because they're looking to move into their dream home. They want a home that is going to be stylish, organised and spacious; a home where there's room to put the washing away and the children's toys don't clutter the living room. To sell a property you have to show a buyer their dream house.

Although the family home only needed tidying up in the living areas, it was the bedrooms that caused the main concern. The children's bedrooms were highly personalised with fantasy football for the boys. One boy's bedroom was a shrine to Chelsea Football Club, one to Liverpool and the third bedroom was Arsenal Football Club. Each bedroom featured football wallpaper, football curtains, football lampshades and football bedding. Every room was overpowering. Buyers would find it difficult to see past the strong colours and the football themes. In a buyer's mind, those bedrooms no longer existed because the décor was overwhelming, so the property was immediately devalued from a five-bed to a two-bed property. If a buyer can't easily see the value in your property then you'll get a low offer price for your home, or the buyer will walk away without making any offer at all.

I hoped that the property would be able to entice buyers with its annexe, a two-bedroom chalet-style building in the grounds of the family home. It could be used as a home office, a teenage retreat or a guest hideaway. There was so much potential to attract prospective buyers.

As soon as I stepped into the annexe, squeezing through the front door, I knew this was a problem. You couldn't see the carpets as the small rooms were stuffed with cardboard boxes pressed against tired and shabby furniture. This beautiful asset had become an oversized eyesore. It was a storage room for junk and clutter that was unloved and forgotten. In this condition, it was devaluing the property and frightening away buyers.

One of the questions you might be thinking is: 'Why didn't the home owners do something about this?' It's because we love our homes and immediately expect others to love them just as much as we do. It works for us so why wouldn't it work for someone else? Also, we've got used to the things in our home, so we stop seeing it objectively. To us it's comfortable, but to a buyer it might look cluttered, dated or a monstrosity.

If you're decorating your home and thinking about selling your property this year, or in the next few years, I recommend that you consider how your interior changes will add value or devalue your property, and how they will attract or rebuff potential buyers in the future.

The main areas that frequently lower the value of a property include: a disappointing first impression, a garish or bland colour scheme, clutter, and a poor use of space.

FIRST IMPRESSIONS:

In modern times, a potential buyer will usually view a property for the first time on the Internet, so you have only a few seconds to make a great first impression. What will make your home stand out against other properties? Your property needs to fulfil the buyer's basic needs of a fair price, good location and sufficient space. Unless the buyer is hoping for a wreck to modernise, the property should look clean, in good condition, welcoming, and have space for their belongings and room to relax. It should also encapsulate the look and style of your potential buyer's dream home, which is a lot to expect from a few photographs on a website.

The Internet is your friend because it's a story book that will help to showcase your property. Photographs on your property listing will attract your ideal buyer, but only if the styling of your property is targeted to reel them in. If your buyer is family-focused then you can style a family living room and beautiful bedrooms. If the buyer is a busy professional then the perfect office space would be enticing, accompanied with space to entertain friends. If each room is styled perfectly to attract your target buyer, it will entice them to book a viewing. You're over the first hurdle.

Once a potential buyer visits your property, you now have to get them to your front door. This is where it's important for your property to be easy to find because many buyers will drive off if they struggle to find the property. A good location map on your particulars, with a light outside your front door to clearly show the name/number of your property at night, is fundamental to get buyers to your front door. You're over the second hurdle.

Now that you've got them to the front door, you need to entice the buyer into your property, setting their expectations and exciting them with what's to come. The exterior of your property needs to be well-maintained so that it looks as if you care about it. Peeling paint, dirty windows and shabby gardens will put off a buyer because your property looks unloved. If a buyer sees maintenance work before they've even stepped over the threshold, they're already knocking money off the asking price to cover any works. If the outside looks unkempt, then it could give your buyers concern that the inside might also be in need of repairs.

You need to create the best first impression, because only then will your potential buyers be excited about seeing your home. Keeping them interested in your property will help you achieve the best offer price and a quick sale.

COLOUR:

From the moment a potential buyer steps into your property, colour flow is critical. If the colour flows from the front of the house to the back of the house, upstairs and downstairs then it will help your home to feel co-ordinated, stylish, spacious and balanced. With no surprises for buyers, it helps them to feel connected to the space which can encourage them to buy your property. Have you ever fallen in love with a property as soon as you've walked in the door? It's because you feel connected to the space. Colour is an amazing tool to help a property feel welcoming and inviting to buyers.

The most profitable colour to sell your property varies depending on the interior fashion of the time, but generally, a neutral front door is balanced with a harmonious colour scheme within the home.

A neutral front door could be white, black, cream, brown, grey or even green. They're easy-to-live-with colours that are non-offensive to the majority of buyers. If you want to disguise the look of dust and dirt, maybe because you live in the country or on a busy street with passing traffic, then it's wise to choose darker shades of these colours. If you have a viewing, I would always recommend a quick wipe over of your front door to make sure it's sparkling for your visiting buyers.

Once a buyer steps into your home, they need to get 'that feeling'. You know the feeling. The one you get when you walk into a property and feel that it's just right for you. It's when a buyer feels so comfortable with the space that they just want to sit down and relax. A harmonious colour scheme can create this feeling because it encourages warm and welcoming emotions. It's the most pleasing and nurturing way to use colour within the home because it creates balance and harmony that's easy to live with.

A harmonious colour scheme uses two colours that are next to each other on the Colour Wheel. The Colour Wheel is a rainbow of colours that are positioned next to each other in a specific order – red, orange, yellow, green, blue and violet. Within interiors, the Colour Wheel is used to determine different colour schemes. There are a plethora of colour schemes, but for selling homes, harmonious is the most successful.

Blue and green are generally the most popular colours chosen for a harmonious colour scheme to help sell a home, blended with a neutral white or cream for balance. Throughout the property, you stick to the same three colours but use them in different percentages in each room. For example, you could have predominantly white and green in the living room with touches of blue accessories, but then swap it over in the bedroom with blue and white bedding balanced with green plants. The colours are the same, giving a feeling of balance and harmony throughout the property, but they're just swapped around to make each room look a little more interesting and individual.

CLUTTER:

One of the things that will instantly devalue a property is a home that looks disorganised. It's not what any buyer wants to see and it will put them off buying your home.

If you show a home that's stuffed to bursting, then it gives an impression that it's too small and cramped for your belongings. The buyer's perception is that if it's too small for you, then it's also going to be too small for them. A home that is organised, from coats and shoes to the laundry and kids' toys, will showcase the space within your property and entice a buyer to make an offer.

Clutter in most properties, consists of three main challenges:

colour too bright and bold, furniture too large or old and worn out, personal things stuffed on shelves or in cupboards. Just because you've put things in a cupboard doesn't necessarily mean that it's organised. There should be space around your things to easily see everything and reach every item. The key is to remember that SPACE SELLS. Every cupboard should look just as lovely on the inside as it does on the outside because a buyer will open your cupboards to see how much space there is for their belongings. If your shelves are bulging then your home is too small for them and they're unlikely to make you a tasty offer.

Moving house is the ideal time to go through your things and dispose of items that are worn out, unloved or not adding value to your life. It's time well spent to stop your property from being devalued. If your home is still bursting with objects, even after you've had a clear-out, then it would be useful to try and put things into storage to try and optimise the amount of space in your home. Maybe you have a garage where you can start to box up the things you won't need in the next few months, or perhaps you have a friend/neighbour who's willing to look after your things until your property sells. The aim is to make your home look organised and as roomy as possible so that it looks like your buyer's dream home.

If you need additional help and guidance on how to organise or declutter your home, refer back to Chapter 3 to master your clutter triggers.

USE OF SPACE:

The majority of homes that are struggling to sell are under-utilised because they don't optimise the available space. I've seen junk rooms, a nothing room and even empty spaces. By not giving each and every space in your home a clearly-defined purpose, you're devaluing your property. A buyer won't be able to identify with the space, so they don't get the emotional connection.

A buyer doesn't want to invest in a junk room. They want to buy a living room, a cinema room, an office, a playroom, a dining room, a family room or a luxury bedroom. Remember that you're selling not just a building but also the dream lifestyle to your potential buyer. Once they feel emotionally attached to your property then they're inclined to make an attractive offer to secure what they perceive to be their ideal home.

To create an emotional connection, each room should have a clear purpose and be styled accordingly. If you're selling a double bedroom, then it needs to have a double bed that's dressed to perfection. If you're selling a dining room, then the dining table and chairs take centre stage instead of being pushed to the side. If you're selling an office or a playroom, then it should be organised with appropriate storage.

Some owners decide to style their property for marketing photos and then quickly remove the furniture and accessories. The property is now incongruent with the buyer's expectations as, from the marketing photographs, they imagined it to be furnished. An unfurnished space is just as off-putting as a cluttered home because it doesn't enable a buyer to imagine themselves living comfortably in the space.

Showing a buyer how every room could be used adds value to your property. As your target buyer wanders around your home, they can easily see how each room could be used to suit them and their lifestyle. They understand how furniture sits within each space and, most importantly, they can see how the building becomes a home. It helps them feel connected to your property, which in turn can entice them to pay more to buy your home.

In summary, when selling your property, the interior needs to meet or exceed your buyer expectations so that it connects to their emotions and creates a desirable home. Once you create their dream home, then a buyer will be enticed to make you the best offer so that you can achieve a sale to move out and move on with your life.

YOUR MEMORIES TO CHERISH

This is your personal space to record the memories you never want to forget. You can take a moment to jot down, draw or scribble your thoughts and ideas.

CHAPTER 7

HOME WORK

Once I'd taken the bold leap to start my own interior design practice, I dreamt of a beautiful office with chic stylish furniture, designer wallpaper and trendy lighting. I imagined that clients would lounge on a modern leather sofa whilst I showcased projects in the luxurious surroundings. It was exciting planning the décor for my dream design office. Every day, I imagined leaving my house and walking in the door of my bright and sparkling office.

Before starting my company, however, I was chatting to one of my design friends who said that she spent most of her time at client sites. A facilitated office was, therefore, both unnecessary and costly. I decided to take her advice and work from home. I was used to leaving the house every day, so how was I going to feel working from home? How was I going to fit an office into my house? And, most importantly, how was I going to separate the two parts of my life to stop work from intruding into family life?

Fortunately, I had a room at the front of my house that I converted into a dedicated office. With a separate room, I'd be close to my children but still able to shut the door and close off work at the end of the day. It had once been my children's playroom so it was full of happy memories, stories and giggles. All of their love and happiness would be the perfect setting for my fledgling business. Now that my children were a little older, the bulky toys had disappeared and they no longer needed a play space. I could claim the playroom as my own. Moving the television into the living room created their relaxing chill-out space. The children didn't mind as long as they had plenty of floor space for my daughter's dancing and my son's train track. They were excited to have a larger, more grown up space and I was excited to have a room defined for my work.

Working previously in a sterile, corporate office environment, I wanted my space to be personalised with colour and pattern. It was something I'd never been able to do before. It felt exciting having the freedom to create my own space, not being dictated by the taste or constraints of others. How would I begin designing a functional and creative design studio?

Around the same time I'd been dabbling in Feng Shui, reading *Practical Feng Shui* by Simon Brown, learning how to influence energy levels in a space through furniture layout, lighting and colour. I found it insightful how energy could be displaced or enhanced in a room. Like the feeling when you walk into a room and it's cold or unwelcoming where energy is dull and stagnant. Or, times when you step inside a room and you feel calm and relaxed because the energy is warm and welcoming.

As I'd be working on my own and ideally wanted a stimulating, inspiring and happy environment, I thought it would be useful to try out the Feng Shui principles on my office. There are different principles of how energy moves in a home, but the primary focus is to balance slow, passive Yin energy, with active, energetic Yang energy. I decided to use *The Compass Method* to determine the colour scheme for the room because it seemed the most logical with my technical background. The compass is used to determine the direction in a home or a room, with specific features judged on their direction from the centre. There are eight directions of the compass and each one experiences a different kind of energy.

Using a small wooden ladybird compass, given to me by my

children after a trip to a museum, the compass method determined that my office should represent the ocean. With this in mind, I selected a calming sea blue colour for my office space. I was a little wary at first because this office was my creative personal space and blue wasn't a natural choice in my colour spectrum. It reminded me of school uniform. It wasn't that I didn't enjoy school, because I had a great time, but I just didn't like the uniform. I had to wear a navy pleated skirt with a starched white cotton shirt, an acrylic navy jumper and a manly yellow tie.

The only good thing about the jumper was that it covered the tie. I hated acrylic. Being brought up with luxurious fabrics and texture, I loathed the squeaky sensation of acrylic against my nails. I still do today. I was always disappointed how it stretched and mis-shaped in my mother's hot wash. My beautiful new jumper now looked like a rag and I always felt scruffy. It felt scratchy and I wanted to wear wool.

It's important to appreciate how colour and texture can evoke memories that are both good and bad. By focusing on positive memories, incorporating colours and textures that you love in your home, it will help to foster feelings of optimism and happiness. This is particularly important when you're working from home, often on your own, because you sometimes need a boost in morale.

With three external walls in my north-facing office, it was a dark and icy room – cold in the summer and freezing in the winter. Although blue was the Feng Shui colour to create my calming and stylish office space, the coolness of the blue was not the best choice because it made the space feel even more cold and lifeless. I tried to work with the colour for quite a while, thinking that I could learn to live with it, but it didn't inspire me. When I walked into my office I didn't think, "Wow, this looks amazing." It felt like the acrylic jumper, not my style and uncomfortable. The colour was correct on the Feng Shui chart, but it didn't take into account my personal taste.

It was useful for me to try out the principles on my own home, and a good lesson learnt, because it led to one of my underlying design principles – your space should be personal and individual to nurture and support you. No matter how much design theory you throw at a room, it will only feel comfortable if it suits you.

For my interior design branding, I'd selected the colour Fuchsia pink because of its feminine, nurturing and motherly qualities. This was the colour that I wanted in my office, big and bold. I wanted my space to feel welcoming, colourful, stylish and elegant. Pink was ideal and something that my hubby would never agree to in the rest of our house. Just the thought of a pink room made me smile.

I scoured many different wallpaper styles and colours, excitedly waiting for the post to arrive each day with samples to delight or disappoint. I wanted something sumptuous and modern, that would excite and motivate me. It would have style and glamour that would take my mind into a world of creativity.

Eventually, I found the perfect floral pink wallpaper with a soft glittery background. It was a traditional pattern with a modern twist and swathes of glamour. It was ideal for my office and made my workspace feel warm and inviting, creating an inspiring backdrop. I still absolutely love it because it gives me a lift and a boost every day. It's like sitting in my secret garden.

I was lucky to be able to convert the children's playroom into my home office, but I know that this is often not achievable in many homes. Not everyone has the luxury to give over a whole room to office space. So, what are your other options available? Sometimes you have a desk in a space under the stairs, you might have to work at one end of the dining table or you could be squashed into the corner of your bedroom.

Steph had a large house but it was also shared with her mother's childcare business. Working from home, with children noisily running around all day, was not conducive to a productive work space for Steph. It was distracting and disturbing, so she decided to create an office in her master bedroom, which was at the top of the house in the loft. When she shut the door, it felt wonderful because she couldn't hear the commotion beneath her.

Although it was useful not having to pack her things away at the end of the working day, the problem she had now was how to disguise the office space in her master bedroom. With a pile of paperwork in front of her, it was creating a constant to-do list that floated through her mind in the middle of the night. It was unsettling and she was having trouble sleeping. Steph wanted to hide the office area so that she could switch off from work and get a better night's sleep.

This is a common problem when squeezing an office into a home. When you're working, you want to focus on your job but, when you've finished work, you want it to become invisible so that you're no longer reminded of it.

For Steph, I recommended creating a partition in her bedroom to separate the work space from the sleeping space. Being L-shaped it was perfectly shaped for splitting the larger space into the main bedroom and the smaller space into a home office. With a non-permanent shelving unit to separate the two areas, it could be removed at any time. Not only did it allow light to pass from one space to the other, but it also provided storage for books, files and personal photos. The bed couldn't be seen from the office area and the desk wasn't visible from the sleeping area. It created an invisibility cloak for each space. Segmenting Steph's bedroom into two separate areas helped her to let go of work, enabling her to sleep soundly and wake feeling refreshed every morning.

Steph loved a dark, inky blue colour so it was blended across the two areas, with definition given to the sleeping area by using geometric feature wallpaper. With the addition of pattern and texture, it gave the sleeping area prominence so that the space was primarily a bedroom in which to relax and unwind. Incorporating different textures into your décor is a subtle way of successfully defining different areas in a room.

Whether you have a separate office in your home, are limited in your bedroom or confined to a table, creating a stylish and invigorating environment for your home office will certainly help you to focus and concentrate. It will organise your space and help to separate work for a balanced lifestyle.

DEFINING A HOME OFFICE

A dedicated workspace that enables you to spread out is a wish list for many. It's not so much the space itself but being able to separate work from home life. When space is tight and life is busy, work can intrude and start to take over your home life. Once this happens, it often brings resentment and anxiety into your personal space that should be relaxing and energising. How do you keep your office and your home separated?

You might have a desk squashed into your bedroom that's unsettling when you sleep, a dining table crowded with paperwork so you now eat meals off your lap, or shelves laden with folders so there's no room for your family photos. Your home is compromised with office stuff, so it can often feel as if you can't get away from work. How do you set up boundaries to create the perfect balance between your personal and work life?

The first consideration is to assess how much space you can realistically set aside for your work environment – a whole room, a table top, a cupboard, an alcove or a shelf? If you give your work a dedicated space, no matter how small it is, then that alone will help to stop it from taking over the rest of your home. I love this quote by Teddy Roosevelt, *"Do what you can, where you are, with what you have."*

In terms of your home office, I recommend that you create a work setting that suits your personality, works with your lifestyle, suits your home and fits into your space. If you do this then it will create a space where you enjoy working and leaves your home tidy at the end of the day. This will help to clear your mind, organise your life and increase your productivity.

SUITS YOUR PERSONALITY:

Office space is often shoehorned into the home, blended in, with no clear definition. Incorporating your personality into your work space, however, will provide individuality and help to set visible boundaries between work and personal time. A great way of incorporating your personality is to choose a colour that's unlike the rest of your décor, so that you feel as if you're in a totally different space.

I have floral pink wallpaper in my home office that my husband wouldn't feel comfortable living with in other rooms. Although I only have to walk a few steps to my home office, the vibrant colour transports me into a different sensory space. It helps me feel creative and cuts the office off physically and emotionally from the rest of my home.

If your office space is small or compromised, then there are still many ways of using colour to help separate work and personal space. If your office is contained in a cupboard then you could add the wow factor with an energetic splash of colour as you open the door. If you're working on the dining room table then it's easy to throw on a tablecloth to add a change of pattern and texture, creating your workspace. If you're sitting on the sofa with your laptop, you could place a vase of flowers on the coffee table to create a change of space. If you don't have a fixed space to work in, then incorporating these semi-permanent objects can give you just enough of a change to make the space feel different. They can reflect different sides of your personality, helping to separate the diverse areas of your life.

WORKS WITH YOUR LIFESTYLE:

I was asked for advice on a home office because Eloise didn't want to work on the dining room table. She was finding it difficult to switch off at the end of her working day. How could she blend her work and personal life without compromising each other? She could have created a separate office space in her guest bedroom, but she wanted to keep it as her calming Zen place for practicing yoga.

Her guest bedroom, however, was cluttered with a large black printer. The problem of what to do with bulky and unsightly home office equipment is a common problem. Relegating the printer to the guest bedroom was a good solution, until Eloise decided that the room was going to be her calming yoga sanctuary.

In smaller properties or when space is tight, interior design is all about compromise as sometimes there isn't a perfect solution. Eloise had two options if she wanted to work from home. She could either convert the guest bedroom to a dedicated office with a sofa bed for visitors, or she could keep her guest bedroom as it was and continue working at the dining room table. With Eloise practicing yoga, balancing energy in her home was my primary focus. She needed space to relax and an invigorating area for her work.

I knew from listening to Eloise, that the guest bedroom was the perfect calming and peaceful space for yoga practice, with the living/dining space for work. When Eloise spoke of the bedroom her voice was gentle and soothing, and when she mentioned the printer in the room she spoke of work pollution. Listening to her tone of voice and hearing her words of resentment, for the office equipment being in her space of sanctuary, helped me to understand her concerns. The guest bedroom was the ideal place for yoga but the printer had to be positioned somewhere else.

Although there have been talks of a paperless office for many years, printers are still ever popular. Eloise was a busy professional woman whose work involved writing and reviewing technical reports, which isn't always easy on a computer screen, so paper printouts were vital for her productivity. The printer had to be repositioned on a shelf in the living/dining room. When you're confronted with an eyesore, such as large electrical equipment, you can detract from it with beautiful décor and accessories, like attractive wallpaper, an eye-catching vase or personal photographs. Refocusing the eye on something more attractive in the room can help disguise any ugly features. Eloise still had to work at the dining room table, but that was the compromise because she now had a dedicated room for practising yoga and the printer was less of a blemish in her home.

When setting up a home office, it's mindful to look at the cause of the problem and not be blinded by the symptoms. For Eloise, the perceived problem of working at the dining table became less of an issue when the real concerns – the eyesore printer and lack of a dedicated space to relax – were addressed. The home now has a clear work and lifestyle balance.

SUITS YOUR HOME:

As I'm writing this chapter, I'm working from my London club because I'm on my way to visit a client. I'm surrounded by other women, working away on their laptops whilst sitting at the small café tables. It's a light and stylish environment where business women can work, in a stimulating space, to get out of the house and connect with others.

Sitting across from me are two women who obviously know each other. They share information about the projects they're working on, but they have separate tables positioned next to each other, providing individual space and privacy. There's just enough room on the marble-topped table for a small laptop, a crystal glass of freshly minted water, a miniature cactus in a white sculptured pot and a trendy mobile phone. Their golden yellow chairs are softly padded with velour for comfort. Easy listening music swathes the room, subtly cutting through any awkward silences and drumming out the London hustle below. It provides just enough space to work comfortably.

The scene is full of style with stimulation from all of the senses: the sparkle of crystal glass to create a special moment; the lull of background music to brighten an afternoon; the luxurious velvet of the chairs so delightfully comfortable; and fresh mint bolstering the London water to provide instant refreshment. It's an exciting space that's motivating and inspiring.

This scene of the two women could easily translate to the kitchen table – a couple of friends working together and setting goals over a coffee – but would it be so luxurious? Would you go to the effort of getting out your best crystal or would you choose the same old mug?

Sometimes, working from home is an afterthought. We perch here or prop ourselves there. It doesn't feel glamorous or exciting. We just get on with it and it can sometimes feel like drudgery. That's when we need our favourite mug to provide a little comfort. On the days when you're feeling a little lacklustre, it's energising to change your environment by adding in special finishing touches that make you feel amazing. That's when you need to get the crystal out.

Interior design isn't only about the large items such as paint, furniture or curtains. I use a phrase that *"Design is in the Detail."* It means that the smaller items, such as accessories, and attention to specific features enhance the interior of your home. It's particularly important to have a stimulating and personal environment when working from home because it can create a positive space and make you feel happy, which in turn helps to boost your productivity.

In my office I have a collection of letters, all the letter G and absolutely gorgeous. They're totally useless as items, but they're my quirky collection of modern and vintage treasures. They add character to my workspace and remind me of cherished memories. As well as looking great, most importantly, the letters encourage me look up at the wall which helps to release neck tension and eye strain after designing on my computer. The break of looking away from the computer screen, to something I enjoy, helps to reset my mind and clear my thoughts. It provides a moment to recalibrate my ideas and keep the creative juices flowing.

When creating your home office, accessories can add a touch of glamour, humour and inspiration to your space. They can help you work productively and keep you feeling healthy.

FITS INTO YOUR SPACE:

Whether you have lots of space or limited space, organising your work area is key for optimising your time and productivity. Just because you have limited space doesn't mean you can't be organised and, vice versa, just because you have lots of space doesn't always correlate to being organised.

Here are my steps to help you create the optimum home office, but each step might need adjusting to suit your individual space.

Step 1: Once you've decided where the work space will be in your home, set out all of your office items in front of you so that you can see what you need to help you work productively. Include electricals like your laptop and printer, paperwork, storage files, stationery and notice boards. If you can't physically unplug electrical or move heavy items then use a photo of the item. When you see this all together, then you can start to prepare the space.

Step 2: Start by clearing the work area and then placing in the furniture (desk, table and chair) and any large storage units (shelves and cupboards). Position your desk so that you're looking at something interesting. Preferably you'd be looking out of a window, but it could also be feature wallpaper or a notice board full of inspiration.

My desk is positioned in the middle of my office facing a window so that I can see my neighbour's garden whilst I'm working. Beautiful floral wallpaper wraps around me as I work so that I feel inspired whenever I look up. I have a double L-shaped desk, with the front section cleared for me to work on, and the side section organised with Perspex drawers, full of stationery that I need to hand when designing. Behind me is a tall shelf unit stacked with wooden boxes. There's a box for each client so that I can quickly and effortlessly throw in ideas and inspiration of fabric samples and photos. Everything I need quickly is close to hand so that it saves me time and effort, enabling me to focus on design projects and to work effectively.

Step 3: Position your electricals next and place them so that they're easy to reach. Don't overstretch the cables or overload extension sockets because it could cause a fire hazard. I appreciate that it can be more costly, but it's safer to get a qualified electrician to add more sockets where you need them. Never compromise on safety in the home.

My desktop computer doesn't sit on top of my desk because that would take up far too much room. The processor is positioned under the side desk, giving me the freedom to stretch out my legs in front. My screen is hung on the wall, over the corner of the two desks, because then I have loads of desk space to spread out plans and sample books.

Step 4: Once you know where you're going to be sitting and in which direction, you can then organise any paperwork, folders and books. Decide what you need to be close by you and the rest can be filed away so that it's out of sight. With paperwork, there are many ways of organising it successfully. You could either store it separately, such as alphabetically or monthly, or you could store it as a bulk item, such as yearly or by topic. It usually varies depending on the type of paperwork you need to file and how you like to access the information.

One of my clients liked her paperwork to be filed alphabetically, however it was a huge effort for her to sort it into the right folders so it was left abandoned in a pile on the desk. When there was so much paperwork that you could no longer see the surface of the desk, she called me in to help her get straight. I recommended changing her filing system so that the paperwork was sorted in bulk, instead of alphabetically, as it would be quicker and easier for her to put things away. As a psychologist, she had loads of paperwork so I created a folder for her professional research and one for each of her projects.

Thinking about my own office paperwork, I've realised that most things I organise are also by bulk – supplier brochures by room, client documents by project and financial information by year. In my office, if I need access to anything quickly, such as supplier brochures or client files, then they're placed on a shelf behind my chair but everything else is hidden away in a cupboard.

Even if your paperwork is filed electronically then it is worth having a review to make sure the information is quick and easy for you to access. Again, I organise my electronic data in bulk, by client or personal projects for the year. At the end of the year, or when a project is finished, it's then deleted or moved to long-term data storage.

Step 5: Once your paperwork is sorted, it's time to organise your stationery. I find clear Perspex boxes the best way to organise mine so that I can see what I have and can find it quickly. Who wants to waste time looking for a paperclip? Keep it organised and you'll be able to spend more time on the things you enjoy.

For my stationery, I have three different units to help organise what would otherwise be a messy collection of oddments. There's a desk tidy for everyday pens, design scale rulers and notepads. Alongside this, I have a clear Perspex drawer unit for specialist drawing pens, scissors, Sellotape (hidden from the kids), calculator, stapler and staples. I also have a set of miniature Perspex drawers for the smaller items, with a drawer for elastic bands and a separate one for paperclips. Being organised like this saves so much time as I can easily see where everything is when I need it.

Whether you have a large or small area, giving yourself a dedicated and organised office space in your home will help to control the amount of mess it creates. As it contains your work, it should help you feel in control and organised. When you want to work you have everything to hand, and when you've finished working you can hide it away and enjoy being at home.

Organising your space to suit you and the way you like to work is your invisibility cloak to an office that doesn't intrude into family life. It will help increase your productivity, giving you more precious time to spend with loved ones.

YOUR MEMORIES TO CHERISH

This is your personal space to record the memories you never want to forget. You can take a moment to jot down, draw or scribble your thoughts and ideas.

CHAPTER 8

THE UNIVERSITY CHALLENGE

Eventually, most children move on and move out. It's an exciting but daunting time for many parents as their lives return to pre-kids status – the independence of time away without a babysitter, opening the fridge to find food inside, and partying all night knowing that you can sleep off a hangover. It's freedom from responsibilities that once dictated your every day, like the morning school timetable, dashing from swimming lessons to football games, and weekends trekking around animal farms and museums of childhood.

But how do homes change once the children move out? Should you keep it the same or reclaim your space?

Before I went to university I had my own bedroom in my parent's house. It was a small single bedroom, at the front of the house, where I would listen to the gentle hum of the cars driving up and down the road outside. It felt comforting and nurturing, away from the hustle and bustle of a busy family. It was my oasis of calm and security.

When I returned from university for the Christmas holiday, just a few months after moving out, my youngest sister had taken over my bedroom. Not only had she claimed my bed but the room had also been redecorated. It was an instant makeover as soon as I left and, as I stood at the bedroom door in shock and surprise, it made me realise that I wouldn't be living at home ever again. My security had been taken away and I no longer had my own special place in the family home.

My parents had given my bedroom to my sister, not because they were happy for me to leave, but because it was a practical decision which meant my sisters no longer had to share a bedroom. Now, my sisters each had a bedroom of their own and I, as a visitor living out of a suitcase, had to bunk down with one of them when I stayed over. I wouldn't have expected my parents to keep my room especially for me, but I was saddened to no longer be involved in family decisions, especially when they involved me. Although I chose to go away to university, I felt like a nomad displaced from my family home.

When my daughter left for university, I remembered those feelings and decided to keep her bedroom exactly the same. Maybe it's because I felt my bedroom had been 'taken' that I wanted her to feel as if she hadn't left the family. It would still be inviting when she returned for the holidays, helping her to feel secure and included. One of her friends asked her to stay at the university digs over the holidays, but she said that she enjoys being at home.

Thinking now about the significance of this reminds me of my father's last words, praising the love and devotion of his family. Subconsciously, this has become one of my priorities, to ensure that family bond is never broken. To make sure my children feel loved and welcomed so that they can have the affection and know the strength of family that I've been blessed with. When my daughter is ready to move out, then I'll claim back the space and create a luxury guest bedroom, but in the meantime I'm happy for her to have the space to call it her own.

I was once asked to contribute to a magazine about how empty-nesters have changed their children's bedrooms once a child has left home. Some of the parents gave answers similar to my own scenario, where a younger sibling had been given the bedroom, but for others, the parents had taken over the space completely. They had been waiting for the child to go so that they could claim back the room and create a space that is in tune with who they are and how they want to live. It's now a guest bedroom, an office or a personal dressing room.

It's not just bedrooms that are changed when children leave the family home. As parents take control of their space, the whole house often undergoes a makeover.

June and Jimmy were like myself, with their second child going to university. They were ready to party and wanted a stylish lounge to entertain their friends. The only problem was the long narrow living room that was an awkward shape and always a struggle for positioning furniture comfortably. June and Jimmy were uncomfortable inviting their friends over, shoehorning them into the space like a party conga.

Two large sofas cut across the belly of the room with a colourful artisan coffee-come-games table placed in the middle. There was little room to move around the space and it felt more like a small crowded waiting room rather than a lively engaging space for entertaining. No matter how I turned and reconfigured the furniture, the room shape was restricting so the furniture felt squashed and compromised.

The space wasn't working and it didn't suit their dream lifestyle, so I had to look elsewhere for a solution. Next to the living room was a large music room; a perfectly proportioned square. With a contented smile, June mentioned that the music room hadn't changed for many years. It was a room where the whole family came together. June and Jimmy wanted it to stay the same because it was stuffed with fond memories – the piano where the children learned to play, the faded curtains punctured with pine needles from the Christmas tree and a stunning view of the manicured garden that was Jimmy's pride and joy.

The music room looked welcoming and comfortable but, although it was full of fond memories, the space wasn't working for the family. As I walked around the room with June, she started to share niggling problems with the space. Despite this being a lovely large room, only half of it was being used. June didn't know how to position the L-shaped sofa so it had been squashed into a corner of the room. It felt cramped. The family could sit and watch the television without it distracting from the garden vista, however, the television had become the focal point instead of the attractive garden. June and Jimmy wanted the garden view to be the main feature of the room but didn't know how to achieve it without disturbing their memories.

The music room felt comfortable and they'd got used to the space around them looking the same. June called it homely. It made her feel safe and secure. She sat in the same chair, her favourite chair, every day because it made her feel calm and relaxed. But, as June and Jimmy were moving from one stage of their life to another, their home needed to change with them. All of those niggling things were becoming increasingly annoying. They felt stuck in time, unable to move forwards but not wanting to lose their past.

June and Jimmy wanted to take back their space, to have it looking lovely for entertaining friends and celebrating their new freedom. They wanted it to look as lovely on the inside as it did from the outside. How was I going to honour their memories whilst creating an environment to celebrate new beginnings and future happiness? The best solution I could see was to swap the two rooms so that the music room would become the entertaining space and the long thin room would become the television room.

The music room was a far better shape for entertaining as the large square space would accommodate their sofas and be positioned with the garden as the feature focus. As an entertaining space, without a television, the amazing outlook would impress their friends and recognise all of the time Jimmy had spent lovingly creating the beautiful view.

The television room would be modernised with a stylish new sofa and linear television unit, making the most of the room's slender proportions. It created a stylish lounge to help the family relax and unwind.

Although the ideas were clear in my head, I knew it was going to be challenging persuading June and Jimmy to swap the rooms over. The music room had become a tribute to the family and it would be difficult to loosen the ties with their existing memories. I decided the best way forwards was to show June and Jimmy a visual design, a picture, of how the rooms would look when finished. As the saying goes, a picture paints a thousand words. It would enable them to see the space and was an ideal starting point.

As expected, June and Jimmy were initially wary about swapping the rooms and unsettling their memories. With the children going to university, the music room was their last link to the children at home. It was understandable that they would feel apprehensive. Having the experience of feeling dislodged from my family when I went to university, I wanted June and Jimmy to understand that any changes would enhance their memories, giving them the opportunity to create a new adventure.

Seeing the changes, June and Jimmy could appreciate how it would help them face the idea of changing memories. They could see how alterations to the music room would create a wonderful entertaining space. Their furniture could spread out, creating a haven for friends to enjoy, and Jimmy's garden would be visually delightful.

There was even space for the piano to remain, nestled in its favourite corner waiting for a party sing-along.

They could also appreciate how a sleek, modern couch was ideal for the long thin television space and were excited at the prospect of a colourful room, full of energy with their retro art, and space to relax together watching a movie.

The changes brought a new energy to the family home, helping June and Jimmy to take a fresh look at their exciting new freedom. They now had a large living space to celebrate family occasions and a place to unwind at the end of a busy day.

When the children came home for holiday, they loved the new rooms. The music room still felt comfortable and welcoming with their mum and dad's old sofas to greet them, but their favourite change was the stylish new television room that they couldn't wait to share with their friends.

They'd all fallen in love with my ideas and now the whole family could relax in style. June and Jimmy could enjoy their freedom creating new memories, confident that the children still felt settled in their family home.

REDEFINING SPACES

Although we think our homes are static, the space is actually constantly evolving as we grow and mature. As our lives are continuously developing, so our relationship with our home changes and matures. Babies and toddlers need a safe space to play, teenagers want a room to sit in privacy, couples look for a love nest and parents search for a sanctuary.

With each new stage of your life, you take the time to reset your goals. You think about where you want to go and who you want to be, but do you rethink the space around you? It's often forgotten and we live surrounded by the past. It's helpful to have memories of the past, but when your life has moved on and your home no longer supports your stage of life then, as my stories throughout this book show, it can lead to physical, mental or emotional stress.

Changing and repurposing a space is often one of the most difficult changes to make to any home. You've often got used to the room as it is, so it's hard to see the space as anything else. There's also the difficulty that you're not starting with a fresh, blank canvas, so there will be elements of the room that you want to incorporate into your new design. It might be that you're keeping a carpet, a fireplace, the curtains, a sofa, a bed, artwork or a family heirloom and you want them to blend seamlessly with the new décor.

If you want to rejuvenate, energise or bring new purpose to a space, it's useful to begin by taking black and white photos of the room. The photos will help you see what the room looks like from an objective perspective, and stripping out colour will help you to see the balance of the room. It should highlight dark and light spots within the room, which will identify problem areas.

Begin by taking a photo of the room, from the door entrance with the door open, looking into the room. This will help you to identify the first thing people see as they enter the room. Remember the phrase: first impressions count. For every area, you're looking to create a great first impression with a vista that looks enticing. It will draw people into the space, creating an attractive scene with a welcoming feeling.

Once you see the focal point, or main feature, as people enter the room you then need to understand the overall space. If you stand in each corner of the room and take a photo of the opposite corner then you'll get an impression of the total room space. You'll be able to assess what works together in the room and also identify those niggling problems. Photos enable you to look objectively at a space, making it easier for you to assess the room, particularly if you're not used to space planning or furniture layout.

Once you understand the space as it currently is, then you can start to determine the changes you want to make. Begin by writing down a couple of words that express how you want your space to feel once the room is finished and looking good. The words that you choose usually flow from your subconscious mind. They're often the words you utter every time you enter the room, "Oh, I wish this room was..." Maybe you want it to feel light and spacious, warm and welcoming, colourful and fun, relaxing and energising, or safe and secure.

The words you choose might not be the same as your partner's, so always make sure that you both write down a couple of words. This can help you understand where you have common thoughts and differing ideas. Men often use the word "practical" whilst women choose "organised". They're similar thoughts but different words.

The words you choose also identify how you can overcome any

problems or issues with your space. For example, if it feels cramped then you'll often want it to be spacious, if it's dark then you'll want it to be light, if it feels bland then you're looking for colour or texture, and if it's a busy home then you might be looking for a relaxing or calming space.

Now that you understand a little more about the space and how you want it to feel, the next step is to decide what will stay and what will go. What's precious and what do you want to keep?

When changing a space, it's helpful to consider how your home functions as a whole, rather than individual rooms. How do you want the space to flow? Do you want each room to have an individual style or would you prefer to create a cohesive space? Think of your home as a story and consider each room as a chapter in the book. The hallway will be the introduction, the living room the main plot and a bedroom will add drama. Each room comes together to tell the story of your life.

For each room, consider if you want everything to stay or whether it's time to move an item to another space. To help you decide, I recommend that you make a list of all the activities for the room. Most rooms are multi-functional: you might have a bedroom that's also your office; it could be a relaxing living room that doubles as an entertaining space; or perhaps it's a kitchen that's also used for dining. Make a list of each activity and then list all of the furniture, lighting and accessories that sit alongside each activity. You can then use this list to identify any corresponding items you already own and also note down where you need to source additional furniture or accessories to complete your design. Remember your story – furniture items are the characters, décor is the backdrop and accessories enhance the plot.

Sometimes large items have to stay in the same place, but for most objects you can try out different placements and layouts to create a refreshing and invigorating space. Re-energize your story.

When deciding on furniture placement, start with positioning the larger pieces of furniture such as the sofa or the bed and then work down to the smaller items in the room. You're now at the point where you can see the space you're working with, you know how you want it to feel and you've also recognised which items you're keeping in the room.

Once you've decided where your furniture will be positioned, it's useful to review the lighting. Ensure that you have the right type of light where you need it. Maybe you need a ceiling light above a dining table, a table lamp that's subdued for an evening glow, and a floor lamp that's directional for reading. It's worth taking a moment to think about the activities in the daytime and the evening, assessing the level of light each activity requires. It's particularly important to review lighting when you're changing the purpose of a room because what suited one room layout won't necessarily be appropriate for another.

Once the furniture and lighting is in position, the next step is to identify the gaps. Those are the items that you don't have and will need to purchase to complete the design makeover. It's time to think about the finishing touches. The artwork and accessories should be aesthetically placed so that they create pockets of interest in the room.

When considering a design for any room, if it tells a story full of emotion then you're creating a stylish as well as a healthy home. Incorporating existing possessions helps to retain sentimental memories from the past, and adding in new pieces can prepare you for a fresh and exciting adventure. You can create the perfect home to enjoy with loved ones and make memories to cherish.

YOUR MEMORIES TO CHERISH

This is your personal space to record the memories you never want to forget. You can take a moment to jot down, draw or scribble your thoughts and ideas.

AFTERWORD

Thank you for taking the time to read my interior design book and personal stories. My aim was to give you a new perspective on interiors. I hope that you now feel empowered with the knowledge of how interior design and emotions connect to create wellness. If you'd like a little visual inspiration, then you can link to my website for some images of the interiors described within these stories: **www.ga-interiors.co.uk/books/hometocherish**

I trust that the stories have filled you with ideas and inspiration to create your own stylish and healthy home. I would appreciate it if you could please spread the word so that others can also experience the joy of *A Home to Cherish*.

Writing this book has given me the time to reflect on my interior design journey. It has helped me realise how the grief shark has given me courage and taken me in a direction that I would never have thought possible before. As I sit writing these final words, crying into my arms, I'm filled with emotions. I'm sad that my father isn't here to share the joy of my achievements, but I'm also feeling blessed that his creativity has been able to shine through me and my children.

If he was here today, I can imagine him in the kitchen making a doorstopper sandwich whilst puffing on his pipe. As I place the book in his hands, he looks up at me in surprise and the widest smile spreads across his face. He's filled with pride, flips the kettle on and makes me a lovely cup of tea.

To show your appreciation, I would be grateful if you could take a few moments to leave a review on Amazon and your thoughts on social media. I'd love to read your comments and hear about the changes you've made to your interiors. Your comments will be invaluable in helping others to find this book and encourage them to create wellness in their own home for a healthier lifestyle.

This isn't the end of our journey together because, if you'd like to be kept up to date with regular design inspiration, including all the latest events and interior trends, then please subscribe to my free *Designer Digest* newsletter at

www.ga-interiors.co.uk/designerdigest

ACKNOWLEDGEMENTS

This book would only be a dream if it wasn't for the motivation and guidance from some very special people. My heartfelt thanks and appreciation goes out to all of you:

Hilda, the first person who said she would buy my book. She kept me focused, knowing that at least one person was interested in reading my stories.

Annie Kaszina, author of *Do You Choose Your Dog More Carefully Than You Choose your Husband*, who kick-started me into thinking I could be an author. At the time it seemed like a crazy thought but, with her encouragement, I've achieved what I thought was impossible.

Caroline Flanagan, author of *Baby-Proof Your Career*, who gave me the courage and inspiration to include my personal story, to honour my father, as the heart of this book. I'm blessed that Caroline became my accountability friend and voice of reason, keeping me focused with monthly catch ups, making sure I was progressing and achieving my goal.

Watling Street Writers (Anthony, Gemma, Harris, Helen, James, Jonny, Niki, Paul, Tracey) who have laughed and cried with me, sharing my rollercoaster of emotions and listening to the bones of my stories. I'm forever grateful for your honesty to nurture my thoughts, your guidance to develop my ideas and your friendship to keep me motivated.

Stephanie Hale, author and founder of Oxford Literary Consultancy. I thank you and your team for expertly editing and publishing my book. You made the whole process, of taking my words and creating a book, simple and effective.

Amanda, Niki and Rachel, my first readers, who I thank for your patience and persistence to churn through draft versions, helping to improve and enhance my stories.

To my **Clients**, who provide me with inspiration and stretch my creativity; I'm blessed with your support and kindness.

Eleanor Alderton, my daughter, whose beautiful photography adorns the front cover. I'm thankful for your creativity, laughter and mumma cuddles. Your love is so precious and you make me proud to be your mother.

Ian and William Alderton, my boys, who encourage me every day to reach for the stars, to take a leap of faith into the unknown and stretch myself beyond my comfort zone. You're always there to catch me and I love you with all my heart.

Deborah, Samantha and Amanda, my sisters, who have shared my grief and felt my heartache. We've been through tough times together and I love you so very much for your support and encouragement.

W.H. Bibby, my father, who gave me the joy of life and sparkle to be different.

May your home be filled with memories to cherish,

Gwendoline x

ABOUT THE AUTHOR

With a BA (Hons) degree in Business Studies, Gwendoline originally built her career as a computer professional for international IT organisations. She enjoyed the technicality, management and people facing aspects of the role, but she was searching for something more creative.

With her father's death within the same breath of her son being born, it was a turning point in her career where managing the grief focused her on a creative journey, towards a new vocation as an interior designer.

Gwendoline is now a professional interior designer, registered with the British Institute of Interior Design (BIID), as well as a House Doctor consultant trained by celebrity designer Ann Maurice. She has developed her interior design practice, GA Interiors, based in Hertfordshire (England), with many of her clients located in the Home Counties and the Royal Borough of Kensington and Chelsea (London).

Concentrating on residential interior design, Gwendoline focuses on creating stylish, elegant and healthy homes. Her designs have been published in UK interior publications such as House Beautiful, Real Homes, Hertfordshire Life and The Sunday Times Home.

As a professional speaker, Gwendoline is frequently sought out to speak at conferences and events on her specialist topics of '*interior design trends*' and '*wellness within interiors*'. She is also an interior design radio correspondent and enjoys sharing her interior knowledge and experiences.

With an interest in psychology, Gwendoline is constantly evolving her knowledge, researching the effects of interiors upon emotions. Keen to exercise, she also brings an awareness of health and wellness into her designs - combining Healthy Body, Healthy Mind and Healthy Home for a Healthy Lifestyle.

Printed in Great Britain
by Amazon